QUANTUM DIMENSIONS OF HEALING

You can heal yourself now

Dr. Robin Starbuck

Drrobinstarbuck.com

QUANTUM DIMENSIONS OF HEALING

You can heal yourself now

ISBN-13:
978-1544960678

ISBN-10:
1544960670

DISCLAIMER:

The author believes that anyone can heal himself by learning about the nature of God and His willingness to meet the needs of mankind - individually and collectively. If a person's hoped-for result has not occurred, the author maintains that said individual may not have yet reached a sufficient level of awareness to establish the necessary contact. Any advice found in this book is not intended to be a replacement for the advice of a medical doctor or other licensed health care professional. I do not assume liability for any harm that results from a decision to forego medical treatment. I cannot personally guarantee that the suggestions given in this book will result in the same outcomes I, or others, have experienced. I am not responsible for the outcomes that result from following the advice given in this book. There is no guarantee that the teaching in this book will lead to healing. While I believe wholeheartedly in divine healing, I also believe in and encourage you to seek standard diagnostic testing and medical treatment if it is indicated.

About the Author

Robin J. Starbuck (Ph.D., New York University) is founder and director of The English School, New York City, as well as former professor and counselor at City College, NYC; Hunter College, NYC; Brooklyn College and New York University.

Her passions include an unshakable assurance that anyone can heal himself, his country and world without any outside help. This ironclad conviction became part of Robin's quest to survive and thrive in a world of abject neglect and dismissiveness. It was her sole responsibility to heal herself of three major diseases when a mere child, before she could go to school.

A lifetime of searching for answers to other life-threatening conditions has taught her more than the average person could ever hope to learn about God's willingness to heal. An overwhelming sense of gratitude for His guidance had prompted Robin to pursue formal education in order to face what was to come in the future, without fully realizing that she was being prepared by God to act as His personal scribe and relate her findings in the area of spiritual healing.

Dr. Robin Starbuck

drrobinstarbuck.com

ALSO BY DR. ROBIN STARBUCK

DR. ROBIN STARBUCK, M.A., Ph.D., NEW YORK UNIVERSITY:

New York University, Ph.D., Linguistics, 1988

New York University, M.A., Linguistics, 1973

Hunter College of CUNY, B.A., English Literature, 1972

Certification: The University of the State of New York - Teacher's license

Honor Society: Phi Delta Kappa, member

PROFESSIONAL AFFILIATIONS:

*** Teachers of English to Speakers of Other Languages (TESOL)

*** New York State (TESOL)

*** National Council of Teachers of English (NCTE)

*** American Educational Research Association (AERA)

*** American Association for Applied Linguistics (AAAL)

*** Variation in Second Language Acquisition (VSLA)

*** Second Language Acquisition Circle (SLAC)

PUBLICATIONS:

*** "The Influence of Emotional Investment on Interlanguage Production, "Miriam R. Eisenstein & Robin J. Starbuck, New York University, U.M.I.

*** "When You Care About What You Say, "Variation in Second Language Acquisition: Psycholinguistic Issues, Multilingual Matters, S. Gass, C. Madden & Selinker, Eds., with M. Eisenstein.

*** "Investment in Topic and Verb System Accuracy of Advanced Second Language Learners." U.M.I. Dissertation. Sponsoring Committee: Professor Miriam R. Eisenstein, Professor Harvey Nadler, Professor John Victor Singler.

The English School of Dr. Robin Starbuck: Conversation Practice in Natural Settings.

The English School of Dr. Robin Starbuck: An In-depth Study of the Verb System in Modern American English.

The English School of Dr. Robin Starbuck: Don't Underestimate the Power of the Adjective!

The English School of Dr. Robin Starbuck: The Deceptively Little Preposition Functions as Stabilizer.

PRESENTATIONS:

"Caring in a Second Language: The Effect of Emotional Investment on L2 Production," San Antonio, Texas.

Teachers of English to Speakers of Other Languages (TESOL) Conference, March, 1989.

"The Effect of Emotion on L2 Grammatical Accuracy," Tarrytown, New York New York State Annual Conference, November 4-6, 1988, with M. Eisenstein.

"Investment in Topic and Verb System Accuracy of Advanced Second Language Learners." University of Michigan, Ann Arbor, Michigan. Variation in Second Language Acquisition Conference, November, 1987.

PROFESSIONAL HISTORY:

1973 - Present. THE ENGLISH SCHOOL, Owner and Director. Teach large ESL classes, small groups, and individual students - usually at School headquarters, but sometimes at embassies, U.N. missions, corporations. Train and hire teachers and assistants.

1989 – 1991, Hunter College of CUNY, New York, New York, Professor, ESL.

1988 – 1989, City College of CUNY, New York, N.Y., Professor, English.

1986 – 1988, Brooklyn College of CUNY, Brooklyn, New York, Professor, ESL.

TRAVEL:

Extensive - Research and practice throughout the U.S., Europe, Middle East and Far East.

Languages: Japanese, Arabic, English, French, Spanish, Greek, Hebrew.

REFERENCES:

Dr. Miriam Eisenstein, New York University, New York, NY, Chairperson, doctoral committee.

Dr. Harvey Nadler, ESL. Program Director, New York University, New York, NY: member, doctoral committee.

Dr. Len Fox, former Director, ESL Program, Brooklyn College, Brooklyn, NY.

https://books.google.com/books?isbn=9027282773

Robert Bayley, Dennis R. Preston – 1996 – Preview – More editions

International Review of Applied Linguistics in Language Teaching 7:11-36. Dusková, Libuse. 1984. Similarity — An aid or hindrance in foreign language learning? Folia Linguistica 18:103-15. Eisenstein, Miriam R., and Robin J. Starbuck.

Variation in second language acquisition – Volume 50 – Page 125

PUBLICATIONS IN ARTICLES:

https://books.google.com/books?isbn=1853590274

Susan M. Gass – 1989 – Snippet view – More editions

The effect of emotional investment on L2 production
MIRIAM R. EISENSTEIN, ROBIN J. STARBUCK

New York University "As research in second language variation has progressed, it has become increasingly apparent that a number of ..."

Current Issues in European Second Language Acquisition ... – Page 192.

https://books.google.com/books?isbn=3823350439

Bernhard Kettemann, Wilfried Wieden – 1993 – Preview – More editions

Eisenstein, Miriam R. & Starbuck, Robin J. (1989), "The effect of emotional investment on L2 production". In: Gass / Madden / Preston / Selinker, eds. (1989), 125 – 137. Felix, Sascha W. (1984), "Maturational Aspects of Universal ..."

RJS: Various publications on LINGUISTIC VARIATION

Second Language Acquisition and Linguistic Variation – Page 174.

Investment in Topic and Verb System Accuracy of Advanced Second Language Learners, by Dr. Robin Starbuck

New York University

Dissertation Information Service, U.M.I.

University Microfilms International

300 N Zeeb Road, Ann Arbor, Michigan 48106.

ACKNOWLEDGMENTS

I would like to take this opportunity to thank the many friends who have inspired me over the years with their insightful articles and comments as well as responses to my posts on facebook and twitter. Many came forth and participated in a number of fact-finding, data-gathering surveys that I sent out to determine the probability of communicating God's willingness to restore His child. I regret that I cannot recall everyone – the number is too great. (Others are acknowledged where they have contributed elsewhere in this book.) Here are some:

Amy Friend, Amber D'ann Picota, Ancil McBarnett, Angie Morales, Ann Ritter, Alice Briggs, Annie Ripley Rimpson, Brian Bauer, Bruce Engel, Bradly Taylor, Carol Anderson, Christel Gast, Christy Castle, Cayce Talbott, Charles M.Matthews, Cindye Coates, Colleen Lindsey Posey, Chrissy Kane, Curtis Artz, David Duncan, Dawn Lauwrens, Diane Maartens, Ding Calvo, Don K.Preston, Derrick Day, Dan Hassett, David Martin Stevens, David Williams, Deann Still, Daniel Anderson, Dalene Feston Ross, David Kamau Njoroge, Donna Raulerson Pickering, Emmanuel Omari, Enejo Adamu, Elizabeth Cain, Erna Atkins, Ernest L. Yates, Eileen Brennan, Enoch Mawutor Yeboah-Mensah, Eugene Maseko, Erlinda Davison, Flora Samuel, Gail Ellis, Heather Creed, Henry Harris, Hormeku Besa Kwasi, Ian Bentley, Ina Hiro, Irene Martines Gonzalez, Isaac Buckman, John Ogbu, Jonathan A. Forgor, Jannette Calderon Hicks, Jacob

Oommen, Jean-Pierre Cote, Joshua Theo Brendon, James Carter, Jeremiah Johnson, Jim Muffo, Joann Price, Jonathan Brennamen, Joy Williams, James Carter, Julienne Chambers, Janet Dawson, Janet Stanley, Jean Rittenberg, Judy Hall, John Kemp, Kay Fairchild, Kent Lindsay, Ken Etter, Karla Tuazon Garcia, Kirk Stephens, Kenneth Gaveni Shivambu, Kim Letterman, Kathy Jane Nolan, Lance Dodd, Leslie Grace Lee Fenlon, Lori Rosen Caplin, Lance Weldgen, Linda Binett, Linda Barnett, Lisa Thompson, , L.D. Mcgee, Lila Cook, Marlon Arevalo, Mary Clifton, Melanie Hull, Mwanga Leonard Arapsotyo, Michael C King, Mike Carter, Monte Les, Monty Dickerson, Mariska Goosen, Martha Hanshaw, Matthew Robert Payne, Matthew Williams, Maureen Coertzen, Muzi Joint Heir Spirit, Norman Reed, Nana Amankwah, Nana Quame Adu Gyamfi I, Olaitan Ajoke, Ozie Wardrick, Prudence Mukosha Manda, Priscilla Msimuko Ngwira, Pamela Haule, Pat Fraser, Philip Obonyo Juna, Ron Menzies, Russ Lewis, Renata Jackson, Robert Blok, Roy Scott, Robert J. Simon, Ron Jones, Robin L. Elliott, Russell Moore Jeti, Sandy Blakely, Sheila Welch-Pelot, Simon Njoroge, Sonny Hanna, Sue Wooldridge Mobley, Sharon Letson, Simeon Edigbe, Stephen Biswas, Stephen Powell, Sunday Isibor, Suzanne Young Gallagher, Tammora Kalis, Tammy Cummings, Tim Kraft, Tony Dollarpound, Tony Ward, Tylene White, Tomsan Kattackal, Ted Nelson, Valerie Baard, Wendi Giles, Yosuke Sugihara, Zuwaira T Vakaron. [Others, who have been quoted elsewhere in the text can be found in EndNotes.]

...

This book is about one thing and one thing only: You ... yes you ... whoever you are ... you can heal your life. In spiritual reality, you've never been harmed ... deliberately or otherwise ... and all the pain and only the pain can be expunged from your memory by God the moment you want to make the connection. There's no such thing as "trying" spiritual healing. Once awakened, there's no return to sleep.

DEDICATION

Quantum Dimensions of Healing is dedicated, from the bottom of my heart, to You, precious Reader, in the hopes of convincing you that you're but a millimeter or a nanosecond from a fulfillment beyond your wildest dreams!

TABLE OF CONTENTS

PREFACE

Life is, at long last, filled to the brim with fulfillment of God's promises, replete with verve and vitality, like never before . . . ever! We have insights now into greater - much, much greater - healings in every arena of human life - thanks to enlightenment from Quantum Physics, but not until after having straightened out some very sensitive, yet vexing - if not downright explosive, religiosity with its defunct and gnarled eschatology.

I hope to show that language - especially as it deals with emotional awareness - plays a significant role in reaching people in need of healing. Through deeply satisfying explanations of what is going on in ourselves, our universe and beyond, we can open our hearts and minds to possibilities that we've never dreamed of before. IF THIS BOOK SUCCEEDS IN OPENING YOUR MIND TO THE FACT THAT ANSWERS EXIST "OUT THERE", it will have accomplished its entire purpose, and the spiritual search will have begun.

Sometimes people are loathe to credit quantum mechanics with being able to explain the multifarious miracles that have occurred and are related in the Bible. They put up a resistance, not realizing that 'explaining' is not tantamount to 'explaining away' the glorious, supernatural aspect of the miraculous. Instead, it is proving this aspect for the benefit of the tightest-wound naysayer on the planet - the scientist!

Even more importantly, the quantum realm lends itself to beautiful mind-expansion, beyond what we could ever hope for, left to our own devices. It reaches out into heretofore untrodden dimensions as easily as we can say "Beam me up, Scotty!" Its ramifications are beyond belief as they lovingly invade our aching bodies, nations and world, with power and permanence.

This book also grapples with the ubiquitous bugaboo: communication breakdowns that would hinder, retard and even destroy any hope of a universal, worldwide healing of all that ails us. I have surveyed and analyzed a number of haunting issues that fight for their very life - their very fleeting life!

I'm not an evangelist or even a healer per se but a person who has endured and proven a great, great deal in the realm of the latter. I don't even do hands-on or me-pray-for-you type of work: quite frankly I just want to see you - of your own accord - get well, fulfilled and happy beyond your wildest dreams. That's all.

A HAPPY PONDERING

It wasn't for a very long period of time but it was a period of time not long ago that I bought into the belief that God was a wrathful, vengeful God waiting to punish his precious child for failing to have gotten to know Him. But this is so utterly unlike the very nature, essence, fullness and wholly divine nature of our God and is nothing more than a very hypnotic false belief which sucks the unwary into tragic misunderstandings, leading to mistaken identity. God is love! That's who he is! That's what he is! Anyone who has missed the mark and failed to grasp what God is and what God wants has simply misunderstood!

Why don't we see more healings and miracles in this day and age? They've been held back unconscionably by religion - all the major religions of the world! With enlightened and fully awakened eschatology, we can divorce ourselves once and for all from the entire mess that religion has gotten mankind into. This topic will be dealt with in greater detail in PART I: Traditional Religion Renounced.

WHY ARE NOT MORE PEOPLE COMING FORTH? Directly on the heels of taking religion-by-rote, i.e., leaving one's relationship with his Creator in the hands of another person, and summarily dismissing it all - kit 'n caboodle, I invite the reader to consider the role that language plays. For you to convey a major breakthrough - or miss the mark of getting across an exciting revelation - from the mundane to the astronomical has everything to do with language use. (See PART II: Communication Glitches.)

PART III should whet your appetite for the glory and splendor that is QUANTUM PHYSICS. Matter itself, i.e., everything you can touch, scoop together, sit on, fly with, anything at all utterly dissipates under the scrutiny of ... well ... yourself, as seen in the light of quantum mechanics.

There is now a crying need to go deeper and farther than we ever thought possible to prepare the tightly closed human mind for the immense hope and promise accorded by quantum physics. To this end, there is much to be gleaned by delving into its rich and fertile fields. We desperately need to have our minds expanded, as we never cease to fall short when it comes to imagining the things of God, who's right there - and here - in every little quark and photon!

YOU CAN HEAL YOURSELF NOW (PART IV) is the crowning glory of this book.

Healing oneself is the surest way to get the job done completely and permanently. After all, it is your body, your relationship, your economics, your nation, your world, your distress - for all intents and purposes, right? Who would know better what needs to be addressed than yourself?

Healing has been the major interest of my entire lifetime as I have been endeavoring to get the explication right in order to share it with people just like you. I kept finding myself closer and closer to an explanation - but never quite an infallible one – until now. It's not exactly a key or secret as much as a focus modification that I know will result in healing and restoration for all concerned.

Not too much stock is placed in turning one's issue(s) over to another person to pray over. Instead, I believe that we all need to be willing to take an active part in bringing about our own much-needed awakening. You do agree that an awakening is what's in order, right?

You (or, your situation) can be healed - far beyond your fondest dreams - because God wants you whole ... and happy ... and free to be all you ever wanted to be, since that's the way He created you. "So God created man in his own image, in the image of God created he him; male and female created he them (Genesis 1:27 KJV). We – you and I – have a right to believe this and enjoy the blessings that it promises. What I need to convince you of is the need to take it much, much further than you've ever thought possible!"

With Love,

Dr. Robin Starbuck

INTRODUCTION - Part A

Dr. Robin Starbuck - Background

We see trillions of stars bursting on the night sky, always as the Creator caused them to be, in sublime perfection and beauty, like a song of victory and harmony for all mankind and we wonder how that same Creator might reach into our little lives and overpower us with His restorative Love ... and healing.

There is a dire need for expansion in our apprehension of God, the Holy Spirit, and His power on earth, in heaven and far, far beyond. We, mere mortals, for the most part, just don't 'get' it – very much to our detriment!

Quantum mechanics comes rushing to our rescue with vindication that progresses from the seemingly nonsensical ... through making a little sense ... to ultimately making perfect sense! The miraculous has happened and our minds have undergone expansion! We need this expanded consciousness to allow miracles a place to unfold, survive and thrive!

It is my hope to present quantum physics in a way that will shed immediate light on why physical, emotional and even economical healings are as natural as setting a course for outer space! Before going too far askew from our intended goal, let's first deal with spiritual healing in this realm!

This book is intended to give you just about the most unbiased insight into modern Christianity – WITHOUT RELIGION – imaginable.

Here are my credentials:

I was born with three crippling diseases going on in my body, vying for attention, making demands that were never met, in need of professional care that never came and receiving nothing but rejection and condemnation when proper attention was sorely needed. I was dismissively informed that it was God who would heal me, so "mum" was the word regarding my appearance and extreme discomfort all the time. Day after day passed by me with my diseases literally eating me up and my job was to conceal this fact so no one would be the wiser.

I had such severe eczema that I clawed myself to smithereens several times every single day! My eyes were so bad that they were nearly swollen shut. I could hardly breathe most of the time because of my chronic and advanced bronchial asthma. While gasping painfully for air, I struggled with just about every allergy known to man ... all the time ... with not the slightest attempt on anyone's part to get me any medical help. I was informed – as if a badge of merit – that I nearly died on a number of occasions.

My problem ... my struggle ... my needs ... and I was just a wee child!   Finally, one day my parents were compelled, by relatives, to take me to the hospital where I guess I was briefly visited by my mother once every three or four days. My condition had been so severe, so ugly - I'm told, that nobody ever took any photos of me. There were the rest of them – my two brothers, father and mother, but none of me.

There were articles of me in the newspapers telling how Robert Starbuck was excused from military duty because he had to stay home and care for his severely ill child, me.

My parents were "religious" folk and sincerely believed that they had put me in God's hands. In short, it was my job to deal with MY situation. They even compelled me to read the Bible every day which in turn set up a kind of bond between us.

I was never accorded the slightest relief from incessant unbearable itching, bronchial asthma with indescribable wheezing and gasping for air as well as full-blown allergic shut-downs brought on by every trigger on the scene. But God was being "explained" to me as my only hope. Needless to say, I took this very, very seriously, for dear life!

My stint in the hospital cleared me up enough to go to school, albeit a year late. I had a gosh-awful time trying to learn as I was so congested all the time that it was hard to see and hear, to say nothing of concentrate!

Needless to say, making friends was nearly out of the question.

I read the Bible day in and day out – remember, my life depended on it! I continued to clear up enough to make a few friends, discover lipstick, boys, cars, and oh, yeah, my mother convinced me to enroll in modeling school. In retrospect I believe it was to "show" the people who had accused them of neglect that I was now some kind of a beauty queen!

But the skin disease, the numerous allergies, the painfully crippling asthma continued to dog me all through school. I had even entered a beauty contest – and really looked the part – after my latest bout with itching and scratching, wheezing and sneezing was over for the day. Every day.

It was my sovereign duty to suffer in private, get everything under control by myself, and reappear to the family as though I were perfectly fine. I'd read the Bible, always taking copious notes, and sometimes reach such a state of spiritual euphoria that I no longer cared about the three persecuting monster diseases I had had since birth. In moments of illumination, I became aware that this nemesis had been forcing me to refrain from going too far off a direct track to a God-awareness heretofore unheard of. In short, I had developed a sensibility that I had never seen before, nor since.

Then I began experiencing healings (discussed in PART IV: You Can Heal Yourself Now) and other miracles all the time in every aspect of my life, except – you guessed it – the final obliteration of The Big Three. They had a greater purpose in MY life. God had been using these severe challenges in my life in a supernatural way as I set out on my own, left small town life forever for the glittering lights of New York City - where temptations came at me from every side! But my close, intimate relation with God prevented me from getting into deep trouble in ways too numerous to count.

Whenever I encountered a proverbial irresistible force, I was always hailed back to God by the Holy Spirit, usually without knowing how or why and my love for Him grew exponentially. People began asking what it was that I had that made me so happy all the time - which confirmed for me that I was on some special assignment from God. I had felt such a deep and abiding sense of Oneness with Him that my own inner conversations were always about 'Us' and 'We' (God and me) – and with great joy! I loved sharing my findings with people, but mostly, I enjoyed being alone with Him.

I listened to Bible recordings hour after hour after hour, not as an intellectual pursuit, but for the Spirit of it. I began to realize an intimacy with God that overwhelmed my whole being. I used to tell my brothers laughingly: "You wanna see what God looks like? You're looking at her!"

INTRODUCTION - Part B

The Reader - YOU!

Once organized religion is summarily dismissed as a viable path to follow (Part I), the next logical question ought to be "What instead?" Perhaps the mysterious, other-worldly, illogical - albeit mathematical - language of quantum physics can be used to ferret out the underpinnings of the otherwise arcane language of man-made religion for a spell.

It is my hope that my very deep and very, very thorough delving into the things of the Spirit, God, will save people a tremendous amount of effort and time as they embark on their own personal healing journey. Just as much as I wouldn't wish my troubles on anyone else, I also wouldn't trade them for the world.

So, how about the main character in this book? Why, that's You, of course! Can you use healing in any aspect of your life? Some kind of physical ailment, or emotional? Maybe financial, or relational? Maybe you still have a dream that you really, really wish to see fulfilled?

The key word there is "see": we need to get you to overcome being shy about seeing yourself in your healed state. You will, of course, want to get to know the Holy Spirit in order to establish a relationship with Him so that you hear Him speak to you in your spirit. It's a wonderful journey to embark upon because nothing makes God happier and He has beautiful gifts to bestow upon you.

You may well be wondering what the Renunciation of traditional religion (Chap 1-5), Communication glitches (Chap 6-8), Quantum mechanics to the rescue (Chap 9-10), and Quantum physics expanding (Chap 11-14) have to do with YOU CAN HEAL YOURSELF NOW (Chap 15-25). Well, keep your shirt on (my mother used to say that to me!); it's all going to come together to make one major point: With a good, strong desire to heal - by learning about Him from whom all healing manifests - you'll make that cherished contact, and healing will become second nature - from the merely physical to the astronomical!

This book has literally taken me many, many years to write because it is such an urgent topic and can only be answered with an expansion of one's consciousness. People just don't look high enough, don't reach deeply enough and don't envision far enough - an understandable self-imposed limitation, given that it's hardly normal in this realm to imagine doing such a thing.

We have access, however, to another realm where healing is the norm: we have access to God. I wondered how I can possibly get the reader, whom I don't know, to think outside of the box - completely outside of the box - and embrace spiritual healing.

Anyone tuned into supernatural healing knows that there is a percentage of such healings that don't last. This is a major interest of this book because we're focusing on the BIG PICTURE: complete success that can be expanded upon, to include world conditions and beyond. So, if our newly healed person hasn't undergone a major change in his thinking, all of the former underpinnings of the malady - physical or national - are still there.

First and foremost, let's get rid of any junk that wrong religious teaching has dumped in our subconscious and go all the way from there to the world of both quantum physics and astrophysics and we will find ourselves ensconced somewhere in between with a beautiful sense of freedom and mobility, health and harmony, peace, joy and love ad infinitum.

MAIN IDEA TO LOOK FOR THROUGHOUT = APPLICATION.

The scientific construct of applying quantum theory for healing purposes is very new but where this is sure to be different is that we will show how you can apply the truths of quantum theory, biblical truths or truths about the nature of God as easily as we apply a salve to a wound.

IF GOD IS IN US ... AND ALL AROUND US ... WHERE WE WERE AND WHERE WE'RE GOING TO, then why not identify ourselves as being at one with

Him? Jesus paid it all. Do you at times doubt it? Do you sometimes find yourself doing your level best to help God get His mission off the ground? Paul tells us in 2 Cor 5:17 that if we're in Christ we're a brand new creature. All the old stuff has passed completely away ... and that, my friend, is that! No more disease, sickness or sin to bind us to satanic beliefs! This new man - our new selfhood - should be explored till the cows come home. We know precious little about our true be-ing in Christ; and yet it's our open door to heaven right here and now!

PART ONE: TRADITIONAL RELIGION RENOUNCED

CHAPTER 1: I hate traditional religion too!

Come here baby.

Let me hold you.

I see you shakin'

From what they told you.

On those dark threats

You been meditating

Just the thought of God and Hell

You're self-medicating!

Trying to kill the demons

Livin' 'tween your ears

Let me tell you truth

That will take away your fears!

LOVE is over every aspect

Of your being. You're OK!

There IS no cruel God of judgement

Hell, NO! NO WAY!

~ Robert Rutherford [1]

There is a pretty good chance that I hate all that religion is, stands for and has done to civilization more than any agnostic or atheist. BUT, I LOVE GOD!!!

How – I ask you how – can a loving God want to punish his own creation for having misunderstood Him? The answer is that He isn't out there just waiting to seize people by the throat for having wandered off!

The most repulsive part of said wrong-minded religiosity is that people are actually congratulating themselves for being among the special chosen few who are going to make it when the time comes and all the rest of us whom they look down upon are going to sizzle and burn with nary a cool drop of relief throughout all eternity, in hell!!

They are so occupied in their superiority (they hope) over the less fortunate ones and so glad to be above and beyond that they have already slated people to be numbered among the misfortunate (their own special enemies).

Scaring people into repenting, i.e., thinking in their own private way, focusing on everything that could not possibly be part of His divine nature, they take pride in being above those un-special, un-called, un-chosen - burning forever in hell - how in the world is that love? How in the world does that measure up to the standard of God? The answer is that it does not. God is love! God IS love! God is LOVE! GOD is love! GOD IS LOVE!!!!

Psychologically speaking, man's tragic flaw is deciding what he must have – without which he's a borderline basket case! Gotta have this much money, this position, this woman, this degree, this level of I don't know what, before he can be happy. He always comes up short. And he's always waiting for a future event, if he's even lucky enough to have a modicum of hope!

But God (love those two words: "But God…!) never intended it to be that way. He gave us – as His image and likeness – the fullness of Himself, as far as we're capable and willing to open our minds to. He lives on the inside of us and takes over all our shortcomings if we'll only let Him.

In the fleshly realm – which most people believe to be the only, or the most relevant – realm, it's extremely difficult to comprehend the magnitude of God [in Whom we live and move and have our being]; but looking beyond the physical realm, we can learn to see that proofs of His ever-presence and omnipotence abound everywhere – exhibited in the most amazing miracles imaginable.

Questions about what happens after death ought to be answered spiritually, but are usually treated as material questions! In the fleeting physical realm, it's anybody's guess; but, stepping into the spiritual realm – where God resides – everything becomes crystal clear. It is the realm of God in which healings and miracles preponderate while the entire so-called material universe loses its fixity.

Alas for the Truth-seeker, however, who finds it extremely difficult to trust that it is the spiritual realm – not the material – that palpitates with verve and solidity: dynamic, impermeable and free!

Turn from your Old Covenant thinking, your Old Covenant reading, your Old Covenant blaming and hating. We have a New Covenant now. Read all about God and His New Covenant. There has been enough suffering in the world. God's glorious kingdom is unfolding before our very eyes. It's advancing …everywhere … and is unstoppable! Perfection here and now! The New Covenant is loving everyone to life!

In traditional theology, people are being turned off in droves! The self-appointed "powers that be" have laid down their law while inspiration, joy and awe are out the window.

What in the bleep is their problem? So, a person messes up badly, obviously misinformed or whatever. Finally like all of us, they die. And the religionistas want them – not to suffer for a million years – but to suffer FOREVER. What in the blazes is up with that???

We, then search for a good, reliable teacher. But let's bear in mind that the moment you put one teacher or pastor on a pedestal you've proven that that person is not worthy of such calling - or at least that your powers of discernment are awry!

IF A TEACHER IS NOT TEACHING YOU TO QUESTION EVERYTHING, INCLUDING HIMSELF, THEN HE'S NOT A TEACHER AT ALL.

A real teacher doesn't exploit impressionable minds by saying anything but "Follow me only as far as I follow Christ!" Teach your students HOW to do their own thinking, discerning and decision-making. It's no feather in your bonnet, oh lofty teacher, to grab your followers by their minds and get them to do your bidding. Teach them that the unfailing power to make perfect decisions lies with God, Who happens to be within THEM!!

Bible students should never be seduced away from doing their own thinking: their own God-aligned thinking is what can - and will - bring everyone to full realization of the Kingdom of Heaven within. How? With the full power of God (not you) on their side, they will learn HOW TO recognize God's voice within them. They won't be preoccupied with all the warring methodologies out there that are vying for attention, but will recognize that to be a real teacher THEY need to sever their allegiance to you and become themselves a Teacher-trainer. Their followers need to be encouraged - not discouraged - to break new ground courageously by studying out the new findings of highly qualified

Bible scholars, rather than huddle around their leader (you).

The Kingdom is advancing: let those impressionable minds who would sooner follow you off a cliff - let them know that they must take their learning beyond you, into the thirtieth century and beyond - way, way beyond!

"A Master teaches essence" offers Dr. Gary Zukav [2] in his groundbreaking masterpiece,

THE DANCING WU LI MASTERS. "When the essence is perceived, he teaches what is necessary to expand the perception. The Wu Li Master does not speak of gravity until the student stands in wonder at the flower petal falling to the ground. He does not speak of laws until the student, of his own, says, "How strange! I drop two stones simultaneously, one heavy and one light, and both of them reach the earth at the same moment!" He does not speak of mathematics until the student says, "There must be a way to express this more simply." In this way, the Wu Li Master dances with his student. The Wu Li Master does not teach, but the student learns. The Wu Li Master always begins at the center, at the heart of the matter....

"Most people believe that physicists are explaining the world. Some physicists even believe that, but the Wu Li Masters know that they are only dancing with it."

You see, God never set up any religion with its inevitable hierarchy of rulers and followers, nor did He perceive us as sinners who needed a Savior. He never even saw His beloved creation as separated from Himself in any way.

Below is a shining example of the underpinnings of accurate exegesis of the most decisive ancient Jewish war that will guide the earnest learner to ferret out the truth wherever it may be found; and, with such spiritual equipping, carry out his due diligence just as far as the unending search will lead him.

Josephus, Flavius (AD37-100), has had a huge impact on recent eschatological findings as he was about as disinterested in religion as any scholar could be. He was an historian of Jewish extraction and a general who participated in a failed attempt to stave off the Roman advances prior to the ultimate destruction of Jerusalem. In Josephus' historical accounts of the Jewish War, he writes:

The End of the Age

"Whereas the war which the Jews made with the Romans hath been the greatest of all those, not only that have been in our times, but, in a manner, of those that ever were heard of; both of those wherein cities have fought against cities, or nations against nations; while some men who were not concerned in the affairs themselves have gotten together vain and contradictory stories by hearsay, and have written them down after a sophistical manner; and while those that were there present have given false accounts of things, and this either out of a humor of flattery to the Romans, or of hatred towards the Jews; and while their writings contain sometimes accusations, and sometimes encomiums, but nowhere the accurate truth of the facts; I have proposed to myself, for the sake of such as live under the government of the Romans, to translate those books into the Greek tongue, which I formerly composed in the language of our country, and sent to the Upper Barbarians; 2 Joseph, the son of Matthias, by birth a Hebrew, a priest also, and one who at first fought against the Romans myself, and was forced to be present at what was done afterwards, [am the author of this work]. 2. Now at the time when this great concussion of affairs happened, the affairs of the Romans were themselves in great disorder.

[Not wanting] to suffer those Greeks and Romans that were not in the wars to be ignorant of these things, and to read either flatteries or fictions, while the Parthians, and the Babylonians, and the remotest Arabians, and those of our nation beyond Euphrates, with the Adiabeni, by my means, knew accurately both whence the war began, what miseries it brought upon us, and after what manner it ended. 3. It is true, these writers have the confidence to call their accounts histories; wherein yet they seem to me to fail of their own purpose, as well as to relate nothing that is sound. For they have a mind to demonstrate the greatness of the Romans, while they still diminish and lessen the actions of the Jews, as not discerning how it cannot be that those must appear to be great who have only conquered those that were little. Nor are they ashamed to overlook the length of the war, the multitude of the Roman forces who so greatly suffered in it, or the might of the commanders, whose great labors about Jerusalem will be deemed inglorious, if what they achieved be reckoned but a small matter. 4. However, I will not go to the other extreme, out of opposition to those men who extol the Romans nor will I determine to raise the actions of my countrymen too high; but I will prosecute the actions of both parties with accuracy."

JOSEPHUS, FLAVIUS [3]

Historian and General in Army

Upon careful scrutiny, the Christian scholar, through extrapolation, deduces that you and I are the New Jerusalem in this day and age:

But you are the ones chosen by God, chosen for the high calling of priestly work, chosen to be a holy people, God's instruments to do his work and speak out for him, to tell others of the night-and-day difference he made for you---from nothing to something, from rejected to accepted.

1 Peter 2:9 MSG [The Message Bible]

CHAPTER 2: A better approach to interpreting the Bible

Exegesis and eisegesis are opposite approaches to reading the Bible, the former keeping its meaning intact while the latter - a bit more creative(!), - fails to preserve the integrity of the scripture. To say, for example that its reference to an eagle must symbolically indicate the United States of America, which, of course, hadn't even existed 2,000 years ago - this is rank eisegesis!

Revelation 8:13 KJV

And I beheld, and heard an angel flying through the midst of heaven, saying with a loud voice, Woe, woe, woe, to the inhabiters of the earth by reason of the other voices of the trumpet of the three angels, which are yet to sound!

What matters?

If you ponder ... deeply ... the kingdom of God and the fact that it's spreading unchecked (it's doing so by virtue of the fact that it's already here) filling every nook and every cranny in every country and nation, then nothing else will matter.

Jesus, himself, was a kind of social misfit! He boldly proclaimed, "See me, see the Father," healing everyone without regard for their status or condition, freed the woman condemned to die for 'her' adultery.

Jesus repeatedly broke the Sabbath and other kosher laws. He turned water into wine and then was blamed for being a drunk with sinners in their homes.

Then here's one of the most bizarre notions perpetrated against mankind:

"When people say 'Jesus took what you deserve.' Really? At what age does a person deserve to be flogged and nailed to a cross? 7 years old? 10? No? How about the dreadful "age of accountability"? 12? So a 12 year old kid deserves to be flogged and nailed to a cross? No? How about 90? Does a kindly old lady deserve to be flogged and nailed to a cross? At what age do you deserve this? This is not how the atonement works nor is it what the early church believed about the cross. Also, people who say "Jesus took what you deserve" usually say you deserve eternal conscious torment, but being flogged and crucified is not eternal conscious torment, so there's another wrench thrown in the spokes of that whole paradigm. At some point when you start actually thinking about this stuff, you start realizing none of it makes sense and you go running back to the early church fathers for a dose of some better news about the gospel."

~ Jacob M. Wright [4]

There IS better news - there's full-blown healing everywhere for everyone in the Bible and in our lives right now. Don Keathley [5] kindly and painstakingly reveals to us:

"JUST SO YOU KNOW: When Jesus said from the cross 'Father forgive them' it was not an opportunity to bow your heads, sing one more verse, pray a prayer and accept an INVITATION, 'Father forgive them' was a unilateral DECLARATION from the Father through the Son in the Spirit of total forgiveness that reached back to the beginning of time and looked forward to all men who would ever live."

AUDIENCE RELEVANCE

I guess we all know that the Bible wasn't, in fact, written to or about us. How about if I qualified my postulation by pointing out that Jesus was dealing solely with national Israel at that time? His now-famous words were never penned with Greeks or other gentiles in mind: Israel was the world that he spoke of, and to.

Oh, but we, non-descendants of the lineage of Abraham, we have received a fully tweaked, greatly improved gospel instead. It's intended for everyone without exception, but didn't make its appearance until Jesus had come back to earth, looking more like a piercing beam of light.

Saul – in spite of all his arrogant abuses on Christians – was the chosen vessel through whom we received the Good News gospel. Jesus beheld 'Paul' where we limited mortals could only see a faltering and treacherous 'Saul'. We soon learn to forgive him though as we imbibe more and infinitely more of God's priceless Gospel.

THE APOSTLE PAUL

What an amazing human being! Brought up under the Old Covenant – the Mosaic Law – he pursued what he felt needed to be done, the extermination of the enemy, i.e., Christians. Can any of us imagine how he felt upon meeting Jesus in person – years after the Lord's resurrection from the grave? If it had been me, I don't know but I think I might have fainted dead away! A lot of good I would have been, right? Dead as a doornail! But I digress.

Jesus asked Paul why he was persecuting Him. You see, persecuting Christ's followers was tantamount to persecuting Him. Paul suddenly found himself completely blind and needed to be guided back into the town where he miraculously got his sight back. Here's where this story begins:

Paul was so profoundly smitten by his encounter with the Lord that it sustained him through unrelenting attacks on his person. Everywhere he went, Paul and his accomplices were severely beaten and/or stoned to within an inch of their lives and then imprisoned – all as a deterrent to their spreading Christianity.

What is most astonishing is the sheer joy Paul found in doing the Lord's bidding without question. If Jesus had said "Jump," Paul would have said "How high?" He did everything at a level of ebullience that must have caused onlookers to conclude that he was insane. He was insanely in love with his Lord and Savior, Christ Jesus. Oh, how I long to have that degree of trust. Nothing else mattered to Paul: he was so humbled by being chosen to carry out his purpose in God's plan.

The trials and tribulations that Paul faced daily were but "a light affliction" to him. Just one of the abuses he endured would have been a major Deal Breaker for me, but Paul goes around singing hymns and praising God.

This brings me to the real part of this story that I was hoping to impress you with: I'm really reluctant to tell you what it is because you are Bound To misconstrue it and miss a hugely important fact of Christianity - I 'GET' Paul. There, I said it. I get him. Flogged, beaten, stoned, were of no event to him. He didn't even have to pray that the stones might be softer in the next town that he was going to. After all, Stephen, the very first martyr, had had the distinct honor of seeing Jesus standing in front of him as he was being stoned to death. Paul would have changed places with Stephen in a heartbeat to die and be with God, but was quite content to stick with his divine assignment. And now we all have the Apostle Paul to thank for the better part of the New Testament.

AND, FROM ANOTHER FAN OF PAUL:

"I have been a traveler for nearly fifty years, and I have found peace, joy, and companionship wherever I have journeyed. In my opinion, the reason I have enjoyed such satisfying experiences around the globe is because I have carried with me the great truth given us by the Master, "Call no man your father upon the earth: for one is your Father, which is in heaven." This truth has been my passport and has been the open sesame to freedom and joy in all countries, for wherever I have traveled, I have consciously remembered that God is the Father, the creative principle, the life of all with whom I come in contact. No one can change the fact that whatever the name, nationality, race, or creed, there is only one God, one Father, and that we are all children of that one Father; but this truth serves only those who consciously remember it, realize it, believe it, and trust it."

Joel S. Goldsmith [6]

Practicing the Presence

I, too, have had similar experiences traveling around the world. The beautiful people that I met everywhere – India, Japan, Egypt, Malaysia, China, Israel, Indonesia, Iran, Iraq, Hong Kong, Korea, Syria, Lebanon, England, Italy, France, Belgium, Germany, Sweden, Switzerland – to name a few, were a mixture of great comradery, adventure and downright intrigue, fraught with danger and divine protection. To say the least, I kept my oneness with my Maker uppermost in thought!

ARE YOU GROWING GRADUALLY or, have you fully grown in your spiritual apprehension? In your walk with Jesus, in your study of the Word, did you or did you not glean understanding little by little, step by step, here a little there a little? And did you not find many corrections along the way where God was finally able to deal with you on a higher level because you had finally completed the levels leading up to it?

Do you know that it is human nature to forget the levels up to it and just expect everyone to measure up to your new level, forgetting that other people have been learning differently than you and not necessarily in an inferior way? They have been learning similar lessons from a whole different vantage point and for all we know they could be way ahead of you!! When you get a great and golden new insight do you ever think just how naive you were about 10 seconds ago? And when you're busy with self-congratulation did it ever occur to you that the other person may be sailing right past you at this very moment?

You thought you had everything all figured out and suddenly you realize that something no longer makes sense. This would be a very good time for you to remember that you are dealing with the realm of the spiritual and we are all mere mortals trying to comprehend the incomprehensible!!!

One word has been jumping out at me really big all morning: DESIRE. I'm talking about a good, godlike desire such as: "I desire to have my thinking made more godlike." Or, "I desire to love people 100% more than I do." Or, "I desire to 'see' spiritually so clearly that I can bring it to bear on everyone with problems."

In my humble opinion (IMHO), this is the kind of desire is the most powerfully effective prayer known to mankind. It has to be with signs following.

The second part of this word jumping out at me is ... please, please, please don't misunderstand ... AS WE TAKE OUR FIRST FEW STEPS to do what we can humanly to fulfill such righteous desires, the Holy Spirit totally takes over and puts everything in place 'in the twinkling of an eye'!

CHAPTER 3: Not in your strength.

Cecil B. de Mille's rendition of "Moses" notwithstanding, Moses knew full well that he was a Jew. (Exo. 1-4; Acts 7:20-25) Furthermore, he was aware that his God-appointed life purpose was to lead his people, the Jews, out of the captivity of the Egyptians. However, Moses, like a lot of us, sought to do the will of God in his own human strength. God had an entirely different plan in mind – that of carrying it out supernaturally. After all, why would God even think in such limiting terms?

When we ask God for something, let us think big – let's imagine beyond human frailties. Moses thought he could use his position and power to carry out God's plan. He even went so far as to kill a man in a display of his own natural strength. It was patently wrong minded, and he paid the price for it. Sometimes it's hard for us to grasp the fact that God doesn't need our "tooling around" as if we ourselves were the Almighty. First, find God's will; then find out what His plan is.

We have an awesome God. Let's be a little bit awesome ourselves by putting everything in God's hands. He is equal to every challenge and worthy of all the glory.

WHEN YOU FIND YOURSELF ASKING THE HARD QUESTIONS, DON'T DESPAIR, your theology and faith are getting an upgrade. It's all good! For example:

"So what happened in the resurrection of Christ? According to Ephesians 2, ALL were made alive together with him, and ALL were raised together with him. Israel was God's "first born" and as Nicodemus should have known, there was coming a time for all Israel to be reborn (See my article The Born Conspiracy: Is Everyone Born Again?) Spiritually speaking that took place at the resurrection of Christ. An awakening took place. As Jesus said those in the graves, or as Daniel would say it, in the dust of the earth... the defeated poor broken disenfranchised scattered Israelites, would hear his voice and because they were raised together with Christ, they would experience the age of new covenant kingdom life.

"That started in the ministry of Jesus but it really blossomed on the day of Pentecost where thousands were gathered together in Jerusalem from the ends of the earth, being regathered into the NC."

Dr. Chuck Crisco [7]

ANewDayDawning

"It's really amazing that the Bible which is supposed to be the best book to open people's eyes to Jesus' finished works and their identity, has become the biggest book of bondage to religious minded people. To the extent that it is easier to teach the ignorant than to teach a religious minded person who has uncontextual knowledge of the bible.

"The religious minded person is not ready to unlearn to relearn new things... He puts God in a box. What an error!

It's really amazing!"

Herty Afia Tilly [8]

Apostle Tony

@ Soul Touch International

A further elucidation of the need to probe a little deeper - on our own - is that such priceless gems as the following are neither found nor comprehended by the altogether unenlightened:

"I have been crucified with Christ. It is no longer I who live, but Christ who lives in me. And the life I now live in the flesh I live by faith in the Son of God, who loved me and gave himself for me." (Galatians 2:20 ESV)

"Nearly all modern English translations say something very similar to the ESV in translating Galatians 2:20. Note the phrase "I live by faith in the Son of God." The only problem is that this is definitely NOT what the original Greek says. Translated accurately, Paul actually said, I live by THE faith OF the Son of God." There is a vast and significant difference between living "by faith in the Son of God" and living "by the faith OF the Son of God."

The faith by which we are to live this new spiritual life is NOT even our faith. It is Jesus' very own faith and confidence that He had and continues to have in the goodness and constant love of His Abba. What a relief for those of us who continually struggle with not having enough faith. It is not about OUR faith. We will never have enough faith. The faith by which we live the Christian life is to be HIS faith, not ours. We live by and from and through the very faith of Jesus. It is Him living His life in us and through us. It is His faith in the goodness of His father, not ours. We are simply invited to enter into and enjoy the eternal intimacy which has always existed between Jesus and His Eternal Abba."

Lee O'Hare [9]

CHAPTER 4: Application - This is Your part

YOU MUST

-A-s-k-

GOD WITHIN YOU

and it shall be

Given YOU;

YOU MUST

EARNESTLY SEEK

GOD

and ye shall find

THAT GOD IS WITHIN;

MAKE THE EFFORT

TO KNOCK,

and it [GOD AWARENESS]

shall be opened unto YOU.

Ask, and it shall be given you; seek, and ye shall find; knock, and it shall be opened unto you: (Mat7:7 KJV)

HOW CAN WE COME AS CLOSE AS HUMANLY POSSIBLE TO SCIENTIFICALLY "PROVING" ANYTHING, I.E., MAKING CLAIMS THAT ARE GENERALIZABLE ?

(a) Models must be testable

(b) Must generate predictions

(c) Predictions must be able to guide the discovery process.

(d) Must not be merely a default position.

(e) Must abolish counter-claim.

(f) Must extend beyond the intractable problems the opposing paradigm faced.

(g) Must deal with all legitimate scientific concerns.

(h) Must demonstrate all evidence supporting the model.

Every now and then

- you'll feel like

You've arrived at last.

- and it's true,

You have.

And, after that

- guess what?

You start learning

- (discovering)

All over again!

...

TRADITIONAL RELIGION MUST BE DISPENSED WITH

Its basis is fear, resulting in gloom and doom. At the time the Bible was written there was plenty of gloom and doom to go around as Jerusalem was about to be decimated. But in this present time we have the grace of God, replacing the wrath of God; so it behooves us to draw closer and closer to a spiritual apprehension of God's precious love.

MAKING THOSE TIMELY CONNECTIONS

When we think in terms of events developing as time goes by, we are subscribing to a 3D construct of ourselves, like the pilot who gives the control tower her location in terms of distance – not only north and east – of a given point, but also advises them of her altitude. This dynamic, according to Newton, and most Christians I know, moves forward in one direction and in one-dimensional time. We need a Big Apple to fall on our collective head to accept the fact that we live in – at least – a four-dimensional realm, borne out by the special theory of relativity in which things do not move forward but remain static and everything that we, in all our prayers, hope for, already exists.

"Two statements at the beginning of Revelation 21 affirm that the new creation exists in dimensions (or their equivalent) entirely independent of the ones we now experience: I saw a new heaven and a new earth, for the first heaven and the first earth had passed away. The old order of things has passed away. He who was seated on the throne said, 'I am making everything new!'"

Dr. Hugh Ross, Ph.D. [10]

Beyond the Cosmos

NOW LET'S SEE IF WE CAN DO SOME FINE-TUNING OURSELVES:

Change "if" to "because"; "seek" to "acknowledge"; "shall appear" to "is realized", etc. THIS IS NOT CHANGING THE MEANING - IT'S RECOGNIZING ITS FULFILLMENT:

Without the constraints of traditional, ritual-laden religions hanging over our head, we're ready to go full-speed forward.

 THE OLD MAN IS DEAD AND GONE. . YOU'RE FREE!! . LIGHT AND LOVE ARE IN YOU!!

If ye then be risen with Christ, seek those things which are above, where Christ sitteth on the right hand of God. [2] Set your affection on things above, not on things on the earth. [3] For ye are dead, and your life is hid with Christ in God. [4] When Christ, who is our life, shall appear, then shall ye also appear with him in glory. [9] Lie not one to another, seeing that ye have put off the old man with his deeds; [10] And have put on the new man, which is renewed in knowledge after the image of him that created him: [11] Where there is neither Greek nor Jew, circumcision nor uncircumcision, Barbarian, Scythian, bond nor free: but Christ is all, and in all. [12] Put on therefore, as the elect of God, holy and beloved, bowels of mercies, kindness, humbleness of mind, meekness, longsuffering; [13] Forbearing one another, and forgiving one another, if any man have a quarrel against any: even as Christ forgave you, so also do ye. [14] And above all these things put on charity, which is the bond of perfectness. [15] And let the peace of God rule in your hearts, to the which also ye are called in one body; and be ye thankful. [16] Let the word of Christ dwell in you richly in all wisdom; teaching and admonishing one another in psalms and hymns and spiritual songs, singing with grace in your hearts to the Lord. [17] And whatsoever ye do in word or deed, do all in the name of the Lord Jesus, giving thanks to God and the Father by him. [23] And whatsoever ye do, do it heartily, as to the Lord, and not unto men; [24] Knowing that of the Lord ye shall receive the reward of the inheritance: for ye serve the Lord Christ.

Colossians 3:1-4, 9-17, 23-24 KJV

COULD PAUL HAVE DONE ANY BETTER?

"If only Paul had been accorded a few amenities in his life - freedom from imprisonment, for example - he could have ... and would have done so very much more," you say?

Yes, he could have.

And he would have.

His impact at that time would have been far more spectacular and far-reaching.

He would have ... because he could have ... healed and restored thousands more.

He would have done everything conceivable, except, perhaps, to write half of the New Testament!!!

WORKING SOMETHING OUT?

With a more enlightened, inspired view of the overall message of the Bible, we can look upon our own hope of glory:

See what had happened, through Jesus' eyes – your real eyes! Did you take that opportunity all the way to where miracles abound? That challenge was and is your open door to greater and ever greater revelation and experience. Humility will take you a --l-o-o-o-ng way!

How long have you been completely committed? With no flipping back and forth, in and out? Do you now think you're the last word in ... everything? Go back to that place where you were vulnerable. God is waiting for you there.

Are there certain places in your mind (Hey, it's just me again, don't worry.)

Certain private places where things just simply are accepted as

"The way things are"?

You see God everywhere …

In everything …

Well, almost!

I want to tell you, if I may …

That's Not Good Enough!!!

It's those little places, little spaces,

That you wanna clear out

'Coz they loom large

At the wrong-est time

Here's what you can do:

'See' God right there

In that scary place

INSTEAD OF

What your frightened mind believes

Because in fact

The Spiritual truth is

The Way Things Really Are!!!

Seeing beyond the punishing constraints of all religion, the so-called here and now, to where heaven and earth meet ... there's nothing quite like it! Literally seeing another's good as MORE important than our own ... this is where Jesus smiles, the "enemy" joyfully surrenders ... and not one person remains unblessed.

Questions about what happens after death ought to be answered spiritually, but are usually treated as material questions! In the fleeting physical realm, it's anybody's guess; but, stepping into the spiritual realm – where God resides – everything becomes crystal clear. It is the realm of God in which healings and miracles preponderate while the entire so-called material universe loses its fixity.

Alas for the Truth-seeker, however, who finds it astronomically difficult to trust that it is the spiritual realm – not the material – that palpitates with verve and solidity: dynamic, impermeable and free!

The "reason" people don't rebuke negative thoughts enough is that they only visit God briefly and sporadically rather than hanging out with Him, getting to know His lingo and His great willingness to be the answer to their every need.

God did not need our permission in order to forgive us! Forgiveness comes from love and God is Love, so the fact is, God does not have to decide to forgive us. If He had to decide to forgive then the possibility to not forgive arises. The thought to forgive or not to forgive never entered God's mind because He is forgiveness! It's His very nature! To ask God to forgive us with these things in mind is to insult God, and no one would do this on purpose, but only out of ignorance, and God has forgiven that also!

Tim Heart [11]

...

HOW LONG DID IT TAKE YOU?

Have you ever

Done everything exactly right...?

You know it was right because

God had told you what to do,

How to do it,

Why and when to do it

And He told you

"Go ahead, do it afraid,

Just do it

Now!"

So you stepped out

And, as God's representative,

You said what needed to be said.

And, BOOM!!

You got blasted for it,

Raked over the coals,

Insulted for your vocabulary,

Insulted for your audacity,

Insulted for your conviction,

Insulted for your obedience,

On and on, ad nauseam!

You had been out there supporting

But took the brunt of the punishment.

My question for you is this:

How long did it take you then

To wake up and realize

You had just stood up

For God?

How long did it take you

To hear

"Well done good and faithful servant!"

And smile?

CHAPTER 5: "Hot Topics" in modern Christianity

There are so many, many hot topics in and surrounding Christianity that are hotly debated all the time. But I am excited to tell you that, upon careful scrutiny, I find that none of them are relevant to healing by God. So, when someone raises the question of where one should stand on these issues (see list in PART II: Communication glitches), I have a simple (!) mnemonic to give them: T.I.A.H.T.T.I.B.W.D.A.Y.I.H.M.O.O.B.N.T.T.N.M.O.I.R.T.H.

"This Is A Hot Topic That Is Being Widely Debated And Yes I Have My Own Opinion But Neither This Topic Nor My Opinion Is Relevant To Healing."

Buddhism says "do the eight-fold path"

Islam says "do the five pillars and live a righteous life"

Hinduism says "adhere to the four yogas"

Judaism says "live by the Law of Moses"

Mormonism says "get baptized and fulfill the church ordinances"

The Watchtower says "serve and obey Jehovah for assurance of salvation"

Roman Catholicism says "do the seven sacraments"

Protestant legalism says "make Jesus Lord of your life and promise to turn from sin"

Jesus says "Done."

WHAT IF Christians were to quit focusing on whether or not their Papa (God) likes hearing them refer to themselves as wretched, and focused rather on the immensity of God's universe, including its seemingly supernatural realms which reveal themselves first on a quantum level and then are explained logically enough so that 'he that hath an ear' can hear and understand!

COURSE CORRECTIONS

(Thanks to Andrew Wommack) [12]

Oh, how I wish I could just simply be a living witness for God – in a flash – but it is a process. I start off in the way I think is most nearly right, but, alas, I go off again and need yet another Course Correction. I'm like an astronaut – Lol!

Just get started on your godly plan. You'll go off course soon enough – that's a given! The next step is to make course corrections.

People just haven't learned enough yet about the ever-presence, the palpableness and the ecstatic joy of the spiritual realm!

All that we see

Or seem

Is a dream within

A dream.

(Edgar Allen Poe) [13]

The entirety of the material world is infinitely less deterministic, less ominous and less fearsome than it seems. Infinitely. We are intended to take charge of it as our inherited right. But we've got to make that quantum leap mentally, emotionally and spiritually to attain the non-linear, non-material, non-aggressive realm of God. Let go of all materialistic striving. Sink deeply into Spirit and you will soar with the angels. Just remember that the "dream" is what we're letting go of: it's the unreal.

IS THE KINGDOM

like an invisible

unrelenting

wholly good

all powerful

all consuming

tsunami

s-l-o-w-l-y

silently

forging

ahead?

Or, is it

already

here?

"Most of us are familiar with religion in one form or another. Religion is simply the universal quest for self-improvement. Grace is different. Grace isn't a bunch of rules for you to keep. And grace is not God's lubricant for greasing the cogs of self effort. Grace is a Person living his life through you. Living under grace is like being married, only more so. It's the adventure of life shared with Christ.

"I hope you can appreciate that I walk a line between preterist and futurist and my aim is to bring all to the table in healthy discussion without insisting we agree on every last point. We're all brothers here."

Paul Ellis [14]

WHY DOES MANKIND INSIST - THOUSANDS OF YEARS AFTER THE FACT - that the Scriptures are written for and about us? Like Jonah in the sea mammal's belly thought about how elucidating it would be for Robin if he drove home the point that he should have gone directly to Nineveh.

Maybe, just maybe, our superheroes of yesteryear were more interested in their mere survival than in relating a miraculous account of God's hand reaching through the parchment to shake a finger at us.

Surely, we can become inspired and edified by reading all about people's journeys God-ward but we mustn't add our own flavor and drama of idolatry. We choose books to read and TV programs to watch that resonate with us: they go inside and tickle our ears from within. And we have the audacity to judge their veracity solely based on our innermosts.

PRETERISM is the belief that at least some of the apocalyptic prophecies in the Bible's book of Revelation have already come to pass and that they occurred within the first century after Jesus' death, no longer to be expected in the future.

PARTIAL PRETERISM, or postmillenialism, maintains that the doctrine of Jesus' Second Coming will follow the millennium - the period (1,000 years) during which Christ would reign on earth [Rev. 20:1–7], while

FULL PRETERISM holds that all the prophecies have been completely fulfilled.

FUTURISM, of course, believes that all of Jesus' prophecies remain to be completed at some time in the future. And millions of debates ensue.

A classic example of a rebuttal to an attack on preterism is Simon Yap's vehement defense:

"Nero was the 6th king. The '8th king' was not a caesar but a general commissioned by Nero to bring order when 4 kings ruled for 2 years after Nero committed suicide and Galba the 7th king ruled for a short while.

"This 8th king is Vespasian. He was the one who commissioned the destruction of Jerusalem. The commission was carried out by his son, Titus.

"People who criticize Preterism should really know their facts before making a fool out of themselves."

Simon Yap [15]

'In the ongoing conversation in the church over the issues of hell, and eternal conscious torment, the topic of the lake of fire comes up constantly. I am regularly asked, "So, you don't believe in a literal lake of fire?"

'My answer is not a complicated one: no, I do not.

'I also do not believe that Jesus literally belongs to a family of livestock known as Artiodactyla (lamb), or that he has a literal first century weapon hanging out of his mouth like a swollen tongue (sword).

'I do not believe that, up in the heavens somewhere resides a literal woman clothed with our nearest star, which has a circumference of 2,713,406 miles, or that the long-dead Jezebel was a regular attendee at the Church of Thyatira.

'I do not believe in literal, seven-headed space dragons, Godzilla-sized scorpions, or that when Jesus returns he will be armed and outfitted with first century, Roman battle tech.

'I don't believe the earth has four literal corners, that heaven's streets are paved with material formed when stars explode into supernovas, and especially not pure gold, which would make it malleable enough to be molded by hand, meaning that anyone of a significant would leave potholes all over the place. Additionally, I do not believe that heaven's gates are literally made from massive pearls, which would require an equally massive Bivalve (oyster, mussel, clam, etc.), as well as equally massive grains of sand that would need to find their way inside of said monster's shell, which would then cause it to coat it in layer after layer of "nacre," until the massive pear was formed.

'My point is that the book of the Revelation is filled, nay, it is *composed of, literally nothing but purposely exaggerated, apocalyptic imagery, that is not intended to be interpreted hyper literally. They are symbols, pointing to greater realities, and to over-literalize them is to miss the point entirely.

'So, no, I don't believe in a literal lake of fire any more than I believe in a literal version of all the other things listed above, and more. I do, however, have some thoughts on what the symbolism might be pointing us to, and you might have some thoughts on it as well.

That is where it begins, and ends. No one can say with absolute certainty what a particular symbol does or does not mean, but we can certainly talk about it, as friends, brothers, and sisters.

Just some thoughts.

Peace.'

Jeff Turner [16]

"Thomas Carlyle: When your mind is stretched by a big idea it will never return to its original shape.

So wouldn't it be awesome...

if God in Christ created one new humanity at the cross?

if everyone was already reconciled, accepted, forgiven and declared right?

if there was no such thing as hell?

if God's love was all inclusive and unconditional?

if the the judgment spoken of was a past event?

if there was no world wide tribulation?

if satan, or the devil was so defeated that spiritual warfare was just shadow-boxing?

if everyone was born again through Jesus' resurrection?

if God was not standing "against" sin, but healing brokenness?

If even one of those ideas were true?

Dr. Chuck Crisco [17]

Anewdaydawning

NOT EVIL AFTER ALL

The world calls

The treatment of

Joseph's brothers

Rank evil.

I'd be inclined to agree

But for one thing:

Had Joseph been alert enough

To realize that God wanted

Him in Egypt?

So many, many times

In my life, I fought bitterly

To maintain the status quo

When God had one wish

And one wish only:

That I GO!!!

What it all boils down to is that we, "mere mortals" are enjoying the tiniest glimpse of God who loves us so much that He literally resides within us: we have bought into the notion that this is no longer true. We point to every spectre on the outside of us as "proof" of the existence of another power when all that we really needed was a bigger ... a much, much bigger view. Let's see if PART THREE: QUANTUM MECHANICS TO THE RESCUE can lend us a little assist. But, before we do, would you mind looking at the real bugaboo that wants to impede our greater comprehension - COMMUNICATION GLITCHES [PART TWO]. See you there!

PART TWO: COMMUNICATION GLITCHES

CHAPTER 6: Even the pros have trouble communicating.

The real culprit in impeding people's understanding of God's power, availability, and total willingness to give us even our wildest, fondest dreams ... is language. It seems next to impossible to truly convey what is in our hearts and what we need the reader to comprehend before being able to reap the benefits of what we're freely offering. Haven't you tried and tried in vain to communicate something of great significance only to find that the listener or reader just plain doesn't get it? What we're going for (God and me!) in this book has the power to literally change the world and yet people can't seem to refrain from underestimating its value.

We as a species can't imagine good enough! When God becomes - not a means to an end - but the End itself then we have taken the very first step in grasping a power bestowed within us for the first time ever!

FILTERS ARE NOT ALWAYS A GOOD THING!

This morning, I held a brand new coffee filter in my hand and stared at it in wonder and amazement, pondering its functionality: its sheer purity and freedom from lint productibility. Coffee grounds, per se, are not for human consumption; but a cup o' joe most certainly is – after it has been filtered through the bitter sediment. Likewise there's a lot of stuff out there that oughtn't be ground up and consumed by our tender, precious minds; yet we harbor many unhealthy biases in our perceptions and beliefs about God.

Filters can also bring major problems into our lives when they block out (filter out) wisdom and sagacious discrimination: those aforementioned pristine filters become tarnished and limp with use and misuse, kind of like reading the Bible with blinders on. Think about it for a moment and I'm sure you'll agree that there is precious little that we can do without some preconceived notion of what's going on. Am I right? We are so filled with surmisings, opinions, biases, judgements – our own personal perspective on how the world ought to be sliced up – that we can hardly hear the word of God thundering in our hearts!

Extracting these noisome filters can be a daunting undertaking: we may know the Bible fairly well, taking into account the culture and time-frame with special attention to audience relevance and yet hold fast to teachings we've gleaned in Sunday school. In other words, we're just as wrong-minded as can be in our approach to hearing the Holy Spirit as we open His book!

We need to release our desire to figure everything out as quickly and painlessly as is humanly possible and let the Holy Spirit take over! God will teach every sincere seeker of truth in a way and time that will dazzle us and with His special touch of the miraculous! Don't take a chance on missing out: we want Him, He wants us.

Let's approach the Good Book with a renewed conviction of having our entire being shaken to the core; let's drop off old traditional mindsets like yesterday's newspapers! What we're reading may have been written at least 2,000 years ago but so much has happened since then. To tell the truth, we'd have to make a concerted effort to get to the point that we can consider ourselves teachable!

COMMANDING RESPECT

I once followed a teacher

Because his insights were

Most revelatory and new

And he commanded a certain

Kind of respect that drew me

To the safety of his

All-knowing wisdom.

I felt so many illusions

Take flight from whence they came.

Noticed too that all the precious

Reverence for God and his Son

Was fast departing as well.

Dear friends, don't get sucked in

To a brand new idol worship.

The Holy Spirit of

Almighty God is capable

Of talking to you quite directly

Up to and until YOU start

To command respect.

There are some people (like me) who enjoy probing deeply into hidden Bible images and meanings. But this is NOT NECESSARY for an intimate relation with God. Nor is it even necessary for gaining knowledge from the Word, found in the Bible. The Holy Spirit is sufficient to guide you in your walk with God and in your study.

"A matter of semantics!" is often used to liberally flout standard English rules when the speaker isn't quite sure where he stands on an issue. Rather than 'fessing up about his ignorance, he blames language (linguistic) distinctions. It boggles the mind how "a matter of semantics" (subtlety of linguistic meaning) can tear people apart whose beliefs are otherwise compatible.

I USED TO HOARD

Written items

Whether my own

Or, other people's

Until I recognized

All this hoarding

Was going nowhere

And that the Writer

Resides within me.

OMG!! What I was in the middle of doing when this precious nugget came to my mind! I "saw" some negative thoughts coming at me and then I heard a Voice - a very familiar Voice - speak, not to me but to them, "Oh no you don't! You're not gonna invade Robin's perfect mind cuz I've got that! She's dwelling in the secret place of the Most High, which means that you, negative thoughts, cannot - I said cannot - enter!!"

"Most of the fundamental ideas of science are essentially simple, and may, as a rule, be expressed in a language comprehensible to everyone." —Albert Einstein [18]

"Even for the physicist the description in plain language will be a criterion of the degree of understanding that has been reached." —Werner Heisenberg [19]

"If you cannot—in the long run—tell everyone what you have been doing, your doing has been worthless." —Erwin Schrödinger [20]

Isidor I. Rabi [21], Nobel Prize winner in Physics and the former Chairman of the Physics Department at Columbia University, wrote:

"We don't teach our students enough of the intellectual content of experiments - their novelty and their capacity for opening new fields…. My own view is that you take these things personally. You do an experiment because your own philosophy makes you want to know the result. It's too hard, and life is too short, to spend your time doing something because someone else has said it's important. You must feel the thing."

EVEN THE PROS HAVE TROUBLE COMMUNICATING!!

"Generally speaking, people can be grouped into two categories of intellectual preference. The first group prefers explorations which require a precision of logical processes. These are the people who become interested in the natural sciences and mathematics. They do not become scientists because of their education, they choose a scientific education because it gratifies their scientific mental set. The second group prefers explorations which involve the intellect in a less logically rigorous manner. These are the people who become interested in the liberal arts. They do not have a liberal arts mentality because of their education, they choose a liberal arts education because it gratifies their liberal arts mental set. Since both groups are intelligent, it is not difficult for members of one group to understand what members of the other group are studying. However, I have discovered a notable communication problem between the two groups. Many times my physicist friends have attempted to explain a concept to me and, in their exasperation, have tried one explanation after another, each one of which sounded (to me) abstract, difficult to grasp, and generally abstruse. When I could comprehend, at last, what they were trying to communicate, inevitably I was surprised to discover that the idea itself was actually quite simple. Conversely, I often have tried to explain a concept in terms which seemed (to me) laudably lucid, but which, to my exasperation, seemed hopelessly vague, ambiguous, and lacking in precision to my physicist friends."

Gary Zukav [22]

THE DANCING WU LI MASTERS

An Overview of the New Physics

I earnestly believe that God will sing over His creation until its culmination when there's no longer a distinction between earth and heaven itself.

We are becoming increasingly more familiar with the construct of types and shadows; but when we extend that awareness first to the subatomic level and then realize that God – in all His vastness – reigns in the realm of the smallest neutron, we will better comprehend how His son, Jesus, could perform the mind-boggling miracles that he did with such ease.

God spoke (sang) in human language but it was clearly from the Spirit. Plain and simple, his utterances had their counterpart – their source – in a dimension beyond our own!

Sounds that we hear actually communicate messages from above and give new meaning to the prayer language known as 'tongues' – a direct communion with a higher realm. So, when you 'hear' the wave of the Holy Spirit in your spirit, it's time – not to freak out – but to rejoice.

CHAPTER 7: Research & analysis

Let's take a look at some communication testing to try to get a handle on where and why communication breaks down. This is where my doctoral training in preparation to do statistical analyses on subjects to determine their mental and emotional environment comes in handy.

Data were gathered from my interactions with students at New York University to determine how invested they were in certain topics of conversation and what it was that would cause them to lose their focus. The following is an ABSTRACT of my Dissertation:

"In recent years it has become evident that the developing interlanguage of the second language learner is both rule governed and variable. A single grammatical or phonological feature may be produced with varying accuracy under conditions which differ in style, register, task, and attention to form. (Tarone [24] 1979, 1985; Sato [25] 1985; Krashen [26] 1982.) additional variables which may influence accuracy have also been noted. James Lantolf [27] (1983), in a preliminary study, discovered grammatical variation which was dependent on the learner's investment in conversation topic. Interestingly, it has also been found that a condition associated with greater accuracy for one form can result in less correct production for another (Tarone [28] 1985).

"This thesis reports on variation in the accuracy of the verb system of 10 non-native English speakers, each conversing with an interviewer on several topics representing a range of personal investment for the speaker. The verb system was chosen for study because it is developmentally central to the language acquisition process and can potentially reveal variability of structures at different stages of acquisition.

"Prior to the interviews, participants listed topics in five areas that they care about and would like to discuss and 5 which they find uninteresting and don't care to talk about. Speakers were advanced level English learners since pilot testing revealed that differences in performance conditioned by topics switch were most salient for these learners. See also Dr. Miriam Eisenstein [29]. Level of English was determined by a cloze test and a writing sample. Learner's ability to monitor under optimal conditions was assessed by presenting each with their writing sample and giving them the opportunity to make any corrections they wish with a colored pen. The pilot also showed that sometimes the most or least "invested" topics come about spontaneously in the course of conversation, so performance on both planned and spontaneous topics was considered.

"Analysis was both quantitative and qualitative and noted the influence of lexical choice, accuracy in form and usage, and corrections and repetitions by the speaker under invested and uninvested conditions. Post hoc discussions with the speakers took advantage of their interpretations of the conversation and associated feelings. Results are discussed in light of variation theory and implications for second language pedagogy."

Robin J.Starbuck, Ph.D. [30]

Doctor of Philosophy, 1988

New York University

SURVEY ON METAMORPHOSIS OF WORDS AND PHRASES:

HEAR YE!! HEAR YE!!

Recently, I put out a "list" of Christian terminology that is undergoing an upgrade. Being a multi-linguist myself (and please don't tell me they have an ointment for that!), I am painfully aware of secular language glitches that just won't quit!

... "I am sure",

... "It must be"

... "It has to be"

... "I know it is"

all denote tentativeness, uncertainty! How in the blazes can we ever be sure? Leave out the adjectival phrases altogether, and simply state your case.

Then we need to take into consideration cultural differences. I wanted to thank a guy for his thoughtfulness, and started to write "you're so sweet". Then I worried that it might not be perceived like Jonathan Swift's Sweetness and Light in Nigeria.

Woe is us. Communication is getting more and more complex despite all the shortcuts that telegraphic, internet language and pictographs afford. Haven't you done the same thing: write - delete - write - delete, and finally go to your gallery and send them a pic instead?

THE GATHERING OF DATA

[Question: What Christian words can you think of that have changed in meaning and are liable to continue to change?]

THE DATA

Evolution, Evolve, Pray, Communion, Law, Circumcision, Grace, Pastor, Evangelist, Obedience, Repentance, Devil, Demon, Satan, Sanctification, Follow, Separate, Religion, Variation, Doctrine, Worship, Man-like God, Forgive, Purgatory, Hell, Giving, Fellowship, Intercession, Truth, Deliverance, Warfare, Resurrection, Sacrifice, Tithe, Sin, Creationism, Charismatic, Orthodox, Submission, Father, Covering, Authority, Spirit, Fidelity, Righteousness, holiness, Salvation, Prayer, Revelation, Finished, Heaven, Covering, Church, Grace, Evangelist, Covenant, Meditate, Sovereign.

EXCELLENT!!!

Robin Starbuck: Excellent! But have the definitions of these terms changed so much that it's difficult to include them in a conversation?

Robin Starbuck: The term "Christian" is a perfect example of a word that has undergone so much reinterpretation that people are no longer sure what it implies or whether they should be identified with it or not.

What is a Christian anymore? Some people who love God with their whole heart are unsure whether they can say I am a Christian or not. Another example is prayer. I know of many, many forms of prayer that I feel just plain don't work.

The definition of so many words have either lost their original meaning or their meanings are rather murky. One respondent queried, "So now that I'm following you correctly, isn't it a lack of solid teaching that creates this kind of discrepancy?"

RJS Response: Bad teaching, the world is shrinking, cultures and languages are colliding, people are getting lazy. In the Japanese language, for example, there are two ways of speaking and writing, the formal and the informal. The question becomes whether or not a new word or phrase becomes standardized and dictionary worthy.

For ESL learners:

HOW NOT TO PLAGIARIZE

With the help of a good dictionary (mine's on my phone), read one sentence or paragraph of your coveted article; then cover it up and tell it or write it completely in your own words. Don't look back to "steal" what the other person wrote. The key is to tell it in your own words because by doing so, your English will improve exponentially!

Remember, plagiarizing is a felony: you could go to jail for it. Lol.

Just not to go too far from the ESL factor: ESL = Students of the English language, who are struggling with grammar, punctuation, vocabulary, etc. I sympathize with you guys and would like to share my first harrowing eye-opener. I had just started college and was studying Spanish at the time. We were given a rather hefty assignment - to write a composition in Spanish - and I was in a bit of a panic to do so. I struggled with my tenses, active/passive modes, hidden meanings of words and expressions - and then finally I begin to write.

It was quite a struggle, I assure you, but once in a while I was able to quote another writer which I did without using quotation marks. In other words I was writing it as if it were my own original writing. Then I had a friend of mine who was a Spanish professor take a look at it. He burst out laughing at my insertions because all of a sudden my Spanish was 100% perfect and it was such a contrast to my own attempts to write. Even though I was mortified at the time (the professor had been my potential fiance!), it had proven to be an invaluable lesson for me after all: I learned to trust my own ability to assimilate and write things from my heart.

ANOTHER FACT-FINDING SURVEY which I asked interested parties to participate in:

"I'm trying to write an article that will be attractive to non-Christians who are interested in healing themselves and others. My strong point is NOT praying for people who don't participate. There's nothing wrong with praying for others, it's just not my strong suit. I'm hoping that I can present the idea of turning to God completely and implicitly for healing without any thought as to whether it is Christian-based or not. Of course, we know that it's all about God, but do we need to hit them with it right off the bat? I'm interested in seeing people get healed and share their experiences without being blocked by a whole lot of religiosity. The problem as I see it is that what they would need to do is to learn all about God because that's where the healing comes from.

"The concept of resting is not easily understood as people's minds and souls are so filled with what is causing their dis-ease. But there is plenty that they can do to ameliorate the situation that has nothing to do with religion nor with simply resting. It has to do with getting to know God, the Healer. There's an exchange that needs to take place, the exchange of their former self-defeating thinking for new and enlightened thinking.

[Thinking quite facetiously that

* If I mention the word 'religion' the unbeliever will run away screaming!

* If I mention the word 'Christian' they may stay but stiffen up and brace themselves for the worst with very little receptivity to offer me.

* If I mention 'God' they may stay and be very, very skeptical but they may at least listen, especially knowing that the topic du jour is HEALING!!]

CHAPTER 8: Further research & discovery

"Another survey, please!

(Still gathering data!)

I say very freely and without qualification that I HATE RELIGION.

I believe that ALL RELIGION is (a) organized and (b) man-made.

People who love God with all their heart and strive to spread the Good News to the world as it yields to the irresistible takeover of the kingdom of God and who preach and teach this glorious unfoldment are not what I would categorize as religious. Having said that, does anyone have a problem with characterizing religion that way?"

A MOST REVEALING RESPONSE came from Mike Childers [31]: "Religion" is nothing more than man, by his own efforts, attempting to gain the approval of God. That is impossible. Christianity is a relationship with God the Father, through His Son Jesus Christ, by the Power of the Holy Spirit. That isn't religion."

Robin Starbuck: Your description is so perfect, Mike, that I'd like to quote you in my article, if I may?

Mike Childers: Please do, by all means, at any time. People are lost and don't know it because they are following a religion which has no answers and no confident assurance.

Mike Childers: "Religion" is an English translation from Koine Greek. "Devotion" would have been much clearer.

Robin Starbuck: I do feel a deep and earnest devotion to God, but not because any organization is telling me to.

Robin Starbuck: James 1:27 NKJV

Pure and undefiled religion before God and the Father is this: to visit orphans and widows in their trouble, and to keep oneself unspotted from the world.

So, PURE AND UNDEFILED RELIGION is not to organize a set of rules and regulations as to how we should conduct our lives, but merely follow Jesus' example of taking care of orphans and widows.

Timothy Pickering [32]: The English word religion is from two Latin words that mean "return to bondage!" - with that I rest my case!!

Mike Childers: Be ye not entangled again in the yoke of bondage ... and that is EXACTLY what the Apostle Paul was writing about! STAND FAST

Mike Childers: ...in the LIBERTY in which Christ has made you FREE!! AMEN Timothy!

Robin Starbuck: So, instead of returning to bondage, we ought to actually think (and pray) for ourselves and let Holy Spirit guide us all the way.

Timothy Pickering: Did not Jesus say He would 'Send' Holy Spirit to be our teacher and to guide us into ALL truth?!? We simply corrupted His system with another where WE can get some glory too.

Robin Starbuck: What a joy it is to wake up to that and say within ourselves 'Thus far and no farther.'

Brenda Mantooth [33]: God is not a religion - He is a relationship - Abba Father - Daddy God ~

Debra Post [34]: The more I seek God...I enter into relationship. I agree that religion is man made. I hate it too but I recognize that when I chose to turn to God for the first time, religion was being offered to me. It was a beginning but thankfully I pushed through the vail of religion and sought after relationship.

Robin Starbuck: Sooo glad you did, Debra. I'm not sure of the statistics here but I'm afraid that most people, when they get sucked into religion, just never escape.

Debra Post: Yes, I think when you see God's laws you start to fall into the trap of doing what is right versus seeing God's love and yet we all desire to know of his love. Religion is "self" focused. After realizing the true nature of God, I can rest and have peace! Praise the Lord! I just get excited even writing about it!

Rita Swartz [35]: Mike Childers, we can't explain it in more simple words but I will put in the word Love as well.

Rita Swartz: Sometimes people say, "If God wants all of us to have a relationship with Him, why didn't He just preprogram us so we would?" But love cannot be preprogrammed. If we were forced to say yes to Jesus, forced to become Christians, this would go against the grain of God's character and the central theme of Christianity—mainly that Jesus' offer is based on love, the purest form of love.

David Dolejs [36]: What we call religion is actually false religion. I hate it too.

John Kemp [37]: My teacher used to say "religion is man reaching up to God to try to bring us to Him. Jesus is God reaching down to us to bring us to Himself".

Stacy Cameron [38]: Nope...And JESUS DIDN'T EITHER... Notice that most of His rebukes were aimed at the "Religious Leaders and Teachers of the LAW" the Rigidity of Religion stifles True Freedom ... All OUR CREATOR WANTED FROM THE BEGINNING WAS ***RELATIONSHIP***

Not these man made self centered constructs of idolatry.

Stacy Cameron: I detest religion too sis.

Robin Starbuck: I have to really SMH wondering why it ever got started.

Barbara Sternal [39]: I have no problem Robin with characterizing religion that way. Too many "Christians" don't know Christianity through Christ and certainly don't act like Jesus has shown them.

Robin Starbuck: That's my whole point Barbara.

Rita Swartz: The thing is not one of us is in a position to judge or condemn and that's the difference. God has given each one of us a free will of choice to seek Him and to believe in Him.

Chris Welch [40]: Brian Zahnd may do now, and Canon Andrew White certainly does because he uses the word root religare covenantally to mean something you bind yourself to.

Dan Beloved Resurreccion [41]: No problem. It's the solution.

Robin Starbuck: Religion has blossomed into a veritable monster!

WHAT DOES "HEALED" ACTUALLY MEAN? [not the dictionary, but the enlightened healer's, definition].

*The dis-eased part(s) of the body are fixed?

* The body is restored and is fully operational?

* The fix is permanent?

----- OR -----

* The sufferer no longer exists as such. He has received the transformational effect of the awareness of God - his own or that of the healer.

Well, the question refers to definition. The first 3 comply with the dictionary's meaning. However as we apply spiritual truths to a condition and that condition disappears, the meaning of "healing" undergoes an evolutionary process. They're all correct, depending on what you're referring to.

HEALING (dictionary [42] definition):

v.tr.

1.

a. To restore to health or soundness; cure: healed the sick patient.

b. To ease or relieve (emotional distress): Only time can heal her grief.

2. To set right; repair: healed the rift between us.

v.intr.

1.

a. To recover from an illness or injury; return to health.

b. To experience relief from emotional distress: gave the grieving family time to heal.

2. To be relieved or eliminated: The rift between them finally healed.

IF THE "HEALING" WERE TRULY PERMANENT, COMPLETE AND TRANSFORMATIONAL, THERE WOULD BE NO RESIDUAL THREAT OF RECURRENCE - OR ANY OTHER PENALTY - AS ALL WOULD BE INCLUDED IN THE PROCESS.

HOW MATURE IS YOUR CONNECTEDNESS WITH GOD?

That could be all that's missing - maybe yearning for a deeper, more intimate, more consistent, relationship with the ONE who has created you exactly as Himself.

LITTLE LESS LANGUAGE

How does this sound to tell a person who is interested in learning how to heal him/herself: "Let's not get bogged down in theological questions. If you want to know how I would approach healing myself, for starters, it's all about knowing God because that's where healing comes from. We'll just avoid all kinds of doctrinal terminology and get you set up where you're communing with the Holy Spirit of God 24/7. Don't battle with evil, don't raise your arms to the heavens, just keep listening to God, in you, as you."?

Of course, there will be some truths that need to be said in order to apply them, such as "God did not create cancer, addictions, poverty, unhappiness, so they cannot - IN SPIRITUAL REALITY - exist." That's more than enough for any sufferer to contend with, without doctrinal mumbo-jumbo. It's tight and it's right. Making contact with God, especially knowing this healing truth, is what has healed millions throughout time.

MEDITATION

alone lifts your consciousness above the intellectual into the 4th dimension.

How can we lift our conscious awareness above human knowledge into the Spiritual (God) realm?

ANSWER: Meditate

"Religion has resulted in the invention of a new meaning for the word "sovereign," which basically means God controls everything. Nothing can happen but what He wills or allows. However, there is nothing in the actual definition that states that. The dictionary defines "sovereign" as, "1. Paramount; supreme. 2. Having supreme rank or power. 3. Independent: a sovereign state. 4. Excellent." None of these definitions means that God controls everything.

"It is assumed that since God is paramount or supreme that nothing can happen without His approval. That is not what the Scriptures teach.

Andrew Wommack [43]" (Thx to Mark Hicks [44]).

Quantum physics and astrophysics have a tremendous impact in the area of EXPANDING ONE'S ABILITY TO

ENVISION OUT OF THE BOX. They don't pretend to be a HEALER per se but when people realize that every atom and every molecule on this plane of existence and on multifarious other planes of existence all belong exclusively to God, then they can start to appreciate just how great He is.

CHAPTER 9: The Study continues ... and concludes.

Testing of New York University Students, to gather data for statistical SPSS [45] analysis for my doctoral dissertation:

"The approach of researchers to investigating second language development has undergone change as the discipline of second language acquisition (SLA) has evolved. While theoretical linguistics have focused on introspection by an ideal speaker here, second language researchers have taken a more empirical approach....

"As research in second language variation has progressed, it has become increasingly apparent that a number of factors can contribute to variability including the possible influence of emotional investment on learners' interlanguage production. To determine the relationship between personal investment in conversation topic and variation in grammatical accuracy of the verb system in the interlanguage of adult ESL learners, this study was designed and an examination was made of second language learners' use of the verb system under two conditions: invested and uninvested....

"Data Analysis

Every verb in the transcripts was listed on a chart with 'page and line' to show its location in the conversation. In addition to background data and cloze scores for each subject, the following information was coded for each verb: tense, meaning, lexical, formation, person, clause, repetition....

"Statistics

Quantitative results were computed using the Statistical Package for the Social Sciences (SPSS, Version X, Nie, et al., 1975). Descriptive statistics were computed for all quantifiable data. Tests to determine the relative statistical significance of production under the two conditions included the use of t tests for accuracy scores and chi square for the distribution of discourse features. In addition to the statistical comparison, a qualitative analysis was performed to describe participants' performance....

"Results and Discussion

The grammatical accuracy of verbs in SLL's oral production in light of their investment in the topic under discussion was measured as follows. The total number of tokens coded was 1,906. The number of verbs produced under the two conditions was not dramatically different. In the uninvested (not emotionally invested) condition 979 verbs were produced by the 10 learners compared to 927 in the invested topic. These figures include repetitions. There were 78 repetitions in the uninvested condition (7.9% of the verbs produced) and 70 repetitions in the invested condition (6.9%)....

"T tests were computed for the following variables under the two conditions: total verbs correct, lexical choice, tense attempted, and tense form. For each of these variables learners scored a higher percentage correct under the uninvested condition. Using a two tailed probability score, these differences were highly significant at below the .001 level. While there were slightly more repetitions in the uninvested condition these were not statistically significant....

"Interestingly, the standard deviations show that there was greater variation in the uninvested condition. This was surprising since Labov and Tyrone had both predicted increased variation in more monitored speech, and less monitoring had been expected when emotional investment was present. If the amount of repetition is an indication of monitoring, there is not a great difference under the two conditions....

"In terms of monitoring as measured by repetitions (which include self corrections), it would be Illuminating to explain the lack of distinction under invested and uninvested conditions. One possible explanation is that because the invested topic was discussed first, monitoring was higher than normal while less monitoring in the uninvested discussion might have been caused by the fatigue of the speaker. This could have obscured a potential difference under the two conditions....

"Conclusions

It is clear from the results of this study that investment in topic correlates with many kinds of differences in the discourse produced by second language speakers. Accuracy rate was significantly lower when subjects conversed on emotionally loaded topics. The extent to which cognitive load is increased by emotional investment and could potentially cause production errors can only be inferred from the data. An additional explanation for accuracy rate is indicated by the different discourse patterns observed including clause types, verb tenses attempted by learners in the invested conditions and their meanings, and lexical choices. The broader range of tenses attempted by learners in the invested condition may be indicative of greater risk-taking and could contribute to an understanding of the lower accuracy rates....

"There were some unexpected findings. Repetitions were not significantly correlated with investment in topic. While repetitions are merely one tangible piece of evidence of monitoring and monitoring can occur without its being manifested by repetitions, The lack of correlations mentioned above could indicate that the role of monitoring requires further investigation....

"Implications

Virtually every ESL task can be reexamined in light of the research on investment in the topic discussed. It is of utmost importance for the investigator to come to grips with the issues involved in determining a truly 'invested' as well as 'uninvested' topic....

"This thesis also indicates the difficulty in determining when a person is truly invested and truly uninvested in the topic of a conversation. This needs to be dealt with further by SLA researchers....

"An important pedagogical implication for oral proficiency testing and perhaps written proficiency as well is brought out in this thesis. In evaluating performance on proficiency exams it is necessary to consider the possibility that the content of an exam may be evoking an emotional response from one student that it may not be evoking from another. If learners have different emotional responses to the content it may be not only their proficiency but also their emotional response to the content that is being measured....

"Many factors can affect interlanguage variability in SLA; and, in light of this thesis, emotional investment in topic should be added to the list....

"Emotional investment in conversation topic is an area in which only the surface has been touched. More in-depth research with larger samples as well as longitudinal investigations will doubtlessly yield even more fruitful insights into this somewhat neglected aspect of variability in second language acquisition....

Let us never again underestimate the role and function of emotion in our efforts to communicate with our every-brother. It's a two-way street that opens out on infinity itself.

You will see in the next two sections of this book (Quantum mechanics to the rescue and Quantum physics expanding) that EMOTION PLAYS A HUGE ROLE IN GOD'S CARRYING OUT HIS MULTI- DIMENSIONAL PURPOSE.

PART THREE: QUANTUM MECHANICS TO THE RESCUE

CHAPTER 10: Seeing from a new perspective - a real God-perspective!

As we have seen in the previous chapter, EMOTION plays a huge role in inter-personal relations - so much so that linguists are furiously trying to isolate and pinpoint what is and what is not an emotional investment! My last book ferreted out, tested, analyzed and reported on this elusive component to human intercourse. We hadn't dealt with whether it was locatable or not, fixed or fleeting, but we most certainly will now! Emotion is starting to look like it's on a par with molecules of matter ... particles of emotion! Did you ever emotionally yearn for something and wind up emoting it into existence? That ought to keep you titillated!

In 1916 Albert Einstein [46] published his famous GENERAL THEORY OF RELATIVITY which reveals that the space-time continuum undergoes a curvature to make way for the law of gravity. His groundbreaking "Theory" explains the motion of the planets as well as the history and expansion of the universe.

"There are only two ways to live your life. One is as though nothing is a miracle. The other is as though everything is a miracle."

—Albert Einstein [47]

CAN YOU IMAGINE?

Imagine something amazingly wonderful! Now imagine something even greater and more glorious. Now go ahead and imagine something indescribably awesome beyond your wildest dreams! For God to fulfill this for you is as easy as slipping through closed doors or multiplying fishes and bread or walking on water! It was a piece of cake!

WHAT IS EXISTENCE?

Light, as we know it, consists of wave-like behavior as well as particle-like behavior which only belong to our interactions with it. Light doesn't have any properties whatsoever of its own: without us, it simply does not exist. This is hard for us to wrap our finite minds around. But let me reiterate: without us, light does not exist. Now I hope you're sitting down for this one – without light, WE don't exist!! In short, our precious world (I'm being facetious) – without us – doesn't exist!

QUANTUM PHYSICS deals with subatomic particles so minute that they cannot be seen with the naked eye and yet everything in our universe consists of them.

"By faith we understand that the worlds were framed by the word of God, so that the things which are seen were not made of things which are visible." (Hebrews 11:3 KJV)

We marvel at the mere thought that Jesus literally walked through walls. Taking a young boy's lunch, Jesus multiplied it exponentially and fed thousands of people. He healed everyone who sought his help and raised the dead on numerous occasions - even including himself! Generally speaking, people tend to file these well-documented cases in the 'don't- understand- and-don't- need- to' file in their minds. But the ramifications of grappling with and comprehending what's going on is staggering! Let's slough off our resistance to have miracles explained scientifically, knowing - as we ought to - that such knowledge doesn't mitigate against the glorious supernatural acts of God: it embraces them by expanding our ability to see infinitely much more!

The MULTI-DIMENSIONAL EXISTENCE of God explains how He can smooth everything out in the blink of an eye. His overwhelming love for us supercedes any victory that may be gleaned by quarreling with one another over theology or philosophy. We just need to lift our sights high enough.

"I don't see how something so strange as quantum physics can help me to get my healing...." you say? Let me remind you, as brought out in Chapter 1, a change of focus would do a world of good. Then, the next step after changing your focus is to stretch that beautiful imagination of yours (discussed in Chapter 5) to 'see' beyond - way beyond - the doctor's report, right smack into the spiritually tangible reality of all things, into the dimension of the heart of God.

Dr. Hugh Ross tells us

"Physicists have uncovered strong evidence that extra dimensions do indeed exist. Yet predating these physics discoveries by more than nineteen hundred years are the words of the prophets and apostles who penned the sixty-six books of the Bible. These ancient authors, under the inspiration of One who exists both in and beyond the universe and the universe's ten space-time dimensions, described phenomena—such as the creation event, miracles, Jesus' post-resurrection capacities, as well as paradoxical doctrines—that require the existence of extra dimensions, or the functional equivalent of extra dimensions. These writers assured their readers that God's ways and thoughts are beyond our human limits, but that "eternity," some unknown reality beyond this universe, is somehow inscribed within us. Now we have the opportunity and the privilege to see from a new perspective—and to integrate—what yesterday's Bible authors and today's physicists affirm about reality beyond the cosmos."

Beyond the Cosmos

Dr. Hugh Ross, Ph.D. [48]

Anyone can discover a personal measuring rod that will reveal whether they are a little bit "off" the center of God's will in learning - and in life - as they start to encounter confusion and even distress, neatly camouflaged as 'normal,' with a proclivity toward an entirely unwelcome dose of mental laziness.

On target, or at the center, however, has us loving every person we can possibly think of with the sweetest, most compassionate knowing imaginable. This supernatural wholly benevolent Love, this compassion, this understanding has precious little to do with human emotions and the like. It's all about God, whose incredible works superceded the natural laws of our present dimension.

THEY'RE VERY CONNECTED

"Why concern oneself so much with the origin and underpinnings of the UNI-VERSE?" you may rightfully ask. The Japanese way of expressing the act of dreaming tells it all: YUME WO MITA (I 'saw' a dream).

In fact, I care very deeply about people who are seeking answers to life-threatening issues in their mundane lives. If they would look up – way, way up – they'd dis-cover that eternal, immortal, omnipotent God has the absolutely perfect spiritual answer to every possible question, and infinitely more. And, when they begin to probe the quantum field, they inevitably find God at the very core of everything! He is, as noted, entirely spiritual, perfect and eternal. Issues being debated, on the other hand, aren't. As a matter of fact, anything less than eternal is as fleeting as a gossamer web.

Jesus acted in a dimension beyond our meager comprehension when he calmed the storm, fed the multitudes, transported himself through locked doors and healed untold millions. Thank God he could and did! His whole demeanor was akin to poetry in motion, coupled with elegant sounds, beyond the likes of Whose beauty is unfathomable.

STRING THEORY: THE ELEGANT UNIVERSE

"Just as the different vibrational patterns of a violin string give rise to different musical notes, the different vibrational patterns of a fundamental string give rise to different masses and force charges. More frantic vibrational patterns have more energy, while less frantic ones have less energy. Thus, according to string theory, the mass of an elementary particle is determined by the energy of the vibrational pattern of its internal string. Heavier particles have internal strings that vibrate more energetically, while lighter particles have internal strings that vibrate less energetically. So we see that, according to string theory, the observed properties of each elementary particle arise because its internal string undergoes a particular resonant vibrational pattern. The "stuff" of all matter and all forces is the same. Each elementary particle is composed of a different string –that is, each particle is a different string –and all strings are absolutely identical. Differences between the particles arise because their respective strings undergo different vibrational patterns. What appears to be different elementary particles are actually different "notes" on a fundamental string. The universe –being composed of an enormous number of these vibrating strings –is akin to a cosmic symphony."

Brian Greene [49]

The Elegant Universe

WELCOME TO THE COSMIC PARTY!!

A cosmic symphony exists in exquisite harmony where the quantum field hosts healing, wholeness and regeneration for us mere mortals, with vibrations pulsating at a perfect frequency – and pitch! It's pretty hard to wrap our brains around, isn't it? And yet right where we see a blob of matter, the subatomic music plays on and on and on. This phenomenon is taking place right here with no help from our comprehension or participation! We need but to find God throughout the Scriptures, sustaining every single vibration of matter in the physical realm. Sometimes invisible, sometimes visible, a set of frequencies is released, resulting in extraordinary sound waves, straight from the heart of a supernatural God.

EXPANDING OUR HEARING OF GOD'S VIBRATIONS

Generated, as it were, by the voice of God to vibrate the different strings of energy that constitute the material world, the Word of God and its powerful impact on our creation requires us to acquaint ourselves with a complexity of the tonality of sounds that it puts forth far beyond anything we've ever heard or imagined. Spilling over into every aspect of our lives, knowledge of that which constitutes our very bodies, quantum mechanics is at the pulse of physical regeneration.

"Quantum Healing didn't set out to cure cancer or Alzheimer's or any other intractable disease. It set out to see the human body, and human existence in general, through wiser eyes. As a scientist I'm passionate about genes and the brain; as a person I'm totally fascinated by the origins of consciousness. Quantum Healing galvanized my intuition that these areas do not have to be separated. They belong together naturally, and once we feel secure that self-awareness is integral to the healthy workings of the body, it will be integral to existence itself. Beyond that, the possibilities are infinite."

—Rudolph Tanzi, Ph.D., [50] is director of the Genetics and Aging Research Unit and vice chair of neurology at Massachusetts General Hospital. He also serves as the Joseph P. and Rose F. Kennedy Professor of Neurology at Harvard Medical School.

Forward to Deepak Chopra's [51]

QUANTUM HEALING

Mr. Tanzi takes great pains to make it perfectly clear that he is not referring to a matter-based paradigm in his discussion of mind-body connection:

"Materialism left out the mind-body connection. Mind isn't material. Yet our thoughts cause our bodies to move, something we take for granted the minute we get out of bed in the morning but which stands as a great mystery. When you break the body down into organs, tissues, and cells, you can't find the slightest trace of a thought, and yet the mind must be related to the body. How? Reductionism left out the holistic nature of the body. Trillions of cells cooperate to sustain one another, acting to preserve overall balance and health. Up to a quadrillion neural connections in the brain generate a microscopic electrical storm, and yet the result is organized thought, not a jumble of static. As skilled as medical science is at dissecting body and brain, it has little to say about the experience of life as a whole, yet that experience impinges directly on who gets sick and who stays well."

Rudolph Tanzi, Ph.D. [52]

Director of the Genetics and Aging Research Unit

Vice chair of neurology

Massachusetts General Hospital.

Joseph P. and Rose F. Kennedy

Professor of Neurology

Harvard Medical School

CHAPTER 11: The Music of the Spheres

THE QUANTUM WORLD, LIKE MATHEMATICS, IS A-FLUTTER WITH MUSIC AND DANCING!!

Do you remember your Pythagorean Theorem back in science class? The ancient Greek philosopher and mathematician from the 6th century BC who spoke about Music of the Spheres, Pythagoras, was the mathematician who set up equations that undergirded the very creation of music.

To Pythagoras, the sun, moon, stars and planets were mystical expressions of music - so strong was the relationship he perceived between geometry, mathematics and music.

ARE YOU, ASTUTE READER, BEGINNING TO NOTICE A DISTINCT CORRELATION BETWEEN THE VARIATION IN LINGUISTIC TOPIC WITH ITS CONCOMITANT EMOTIONAL INVESTMENT AND THE VARIATION IN THE VIBRATIONS OF THE STRINGS THAT COMPRISE THE "MATERIAL" ASPECT OF OUR UNI-VERSE? AND, OF COURSE, YOU KNOW WHO IT IS THAT KEEPS THESE STRINGS VIBRATING, RIGHT?

Strings, of course, vibrate at different frequencies and each unique frequency determines what sort of subatomic particle they become. Elementary particles aren't points, but vibrating strings as different harmonics correspond to different elementary particles. It is claimed that all elementary particles such as electrons, photons, neutrinos and quarks owe their entire existence to variations in the musical behavior of the strings!

Did you also once believe, as I did, that there was no place for God in physics? If so, you weren't alone; but now we know better - the Bible supports string theory because of its allusions to extra-dimensionality and elegant design.

There is a symbiotic relationship between Spirit, God, and the strings that are nature at its very smallest component.

A good buddy of mine, Frank Hanks, once playfully wrote: "I like that E=MC2 stuff that happens in the spirit. Time loses its effect on matter as light explodes in my spirit, birthing miracles directly from the unseen real outside of time. Things which appear are not made of themselves but are created from substance just beyond the veil where the great high priest over the house of God has His continuing ministry. He loves it when we breach the divide and bring back the power of the kingdom."

Frank Hanks [53]

Author, Publisher and Director at

Empty Hospitals Publishing

"I empty the world's hospitals by training others to heal the sick."FH

THIS WILL ROCK YOUR WORLD IF YOUR WORLD IS STILL
ROCKABLE!!

Subatomic building blocks

"The Scriptures reveal that "what we now see did not
come from anything that can be seen."(Hebrews 11:3
NLT) Many extraordinarily brilliant quantum physicists
believe that the "particles" that constitute the interior
world of the atom are themselves created from invisible
vibrating strings of energy in such a manner that they
eventually coalesced into matter. All of this was
conceived in the mind of God and brought to expression
through the creative command of God. "God said, 'Let
there be light and there was light!'" Light itself consists
of waves of electromagnetic energy that "vibrate" at an
extraordinarily high frequency. If string theory is an
accurate description of the smallest building blocks of
matter, these vibrating strings of energy (and the subatomic particles they eventually constructed) were
brought into being at the command of God as the
foundational building blocks of matter. Because they
were designed by God they could also be uniquely
sustained by the Word of God through the energizing
power of the Holy Spirit. The quantum world has been
intentionally designed to obey the voice of God."

Phil Mason [54]

Quantum Glory

The Science of

Heaven Invading Earth

...

Light is flirtatious by nature - now here, now there, but never pinpoint-able: sometimes a point and sometimes a wave. We tried and tried: first a wiggly wave, then a tenacious dot! Such was the nature of our elusive beam of light, but now we've got it! Or, have we? A photo may be worth a thousand words but we need several million words to interpret the still inexplicable.

Annette Capps, instead of trying to to rein in that elusive dot, ferrets out many, many more equally mind-boggling QUESTIONS!!

"Scientists have performed experiments with atoms and their subatomic particles such as electrons. If you paid attention in school, you saw the diagram of an atom with the electron orbiting it like the earth orbits the sun. The interesting thing is that scientists have discovered that the electron that is shown orbiting the nucleus is not always there in particle form. It exists in a wave state (like a cloud, everywhere at once) until someone looks at it. When the scientist observes it, it suddenly appears as a dot (particle). What we all want to know, is, "How does it know someone is looking at it?" It obviously is responding to the observer's interaction with it."

Annette Capps [55]

Quantum Faith

IF STRINGS WERE TO QUIT VIBRATING,

...would the world collapse all around us? Not if we understand and trust God and His extra-dimensionality. [Please note: I'm not saying, humanly speaking, that our meager mental participation is required to keep the world from imploding! But trusting God in all His multi-dimensionality will bring us into awareness of what is really going on!] The Word of God and the vibrating strings of energy are believed by some physicists to literally constitute the universe, making string theory very attractive to theologians. Phil Mason brilliantly piques our curiosity with his argument that, in fact, God is at the helm:

"It substantiates something which is the very currency of biblical revelation. If string theory is correct, God sustains the entire physical universe by vibrating the very strings of energy that He created by the word of His power. If the strings were to stop vibrating the entire universe would collapse because these strings of vibrating energy are the building blocks of sub-atomic particles and sub-atomic particles are the building blocks of matter. The one thing that string theorists never discuss is what causes the strings to vibrate! Why would a string just continue to vibrate forever unless it was being energized externally from another source of energy? This is one of the mysteries that emerge from string theory, but it is powerfully addressed by the revelation of the sustaining voice of God."

Quantum Glory

The Science of

Heaven Invading Earth

Phil Mason [56]

YOU'RE REALLY GONNA WANT TO ANSWER THIS QUESTION : WHAT CAUSES STRINGS (MATTER) TO VIBRATE WITHOUT EVER STOPPING?

Years ago I concluded, upon having read the major literature on physics, quantum mechanics, and string theory, that God is truly pan-dimensional infinity, the Creator of all the dimensions that are out there as well as within.

EXTRA-DIMENSIONAL HEALING.

I just want you to know that I am PAINFULLY AWARE of what it's like to be wracked with pain: my story(-ies) are far too long and too painful to relate.

...

I KNOW WITH EVERY FIBER OF MY BEING how much one DOESN'T want to hear victory stories when they're at rock bottom. I get it. It's entirely normal. At least it's 'normal' on this plane. Can you at least acknowledge that this isn't the only plane that exists?

Do you believe that Jesus walked right through walls? Can you imagine his whole body, including his garment, at his command?

Far-fetched? Long ago? Stay with me, please. In another dimension, Jesus' many miraculous feats were - and are - a piece of cake! Well, that dimension is right here. We don't have to travel and we don't have to die in order to avail ourselves of God's supernatural power. Reading the Bible with this in mind, with gleaning the inspired Word alone, will bring you to the same place: God, Spirit, Love is all-powerful and right here where we are!!

WHAT TO DO? Let God speak to you. You've got to be VERY, VERY STILL. The Holy Spirit has extremely good news for you: what in the world is more important - to be focused on exclusively - than that?

DO YOU HAVE PAIN IN YOUR (MATERIAL) BODY? HAVE YOU BEEN ORDERING IT TO LEAVE? PROBLEM IS -Y-O-U- '-R-E- NOT CONVINCED THAT YOU HAVE POWER OVER MATTER, RIGHT ? . SEE WHAT ONE FAMOUS PHYSICIST, MAX PLANCK, CONFESSES ABOUT THE STRENGTH AND DOMINION OF MATTER:

"As a man who has devoted his whole life to the most clear headed science, to the study of matter, I can tell you this much as a result of my research about atoms: There is no matter as such. All matter originates and exists only by virtue of a force which brings the particle of an atom to vibration and holds this most minute solar system of the atom together. We must assume behind this force the existence of a conscious and intelligent Mind. This Mind is the matrix of all matter."

Max Planck, 1944 [57]

Nobel Peace Prize winner

Florence, Italy (speech)

"The Nature of Matter"

"THERE IS NO MATTER as such!"

Max Planck [58]

Dimension of the glory realm

HOW WOULD YOU LIKE TO SUPERNATURALLY CROSS OVER into a dimension of the glory realm that's only available to those of us who are willing to give up our entire life to be overtaken by the spiritual life of God?

Phil Mason [59], in his ground-breaking masterpiece, QUANTUM GLORY, writes about a man who has lived a life of apostolic signs and wonders: "Smith Wigglesworth, who by many accounts is regarded as one of the most anointed men of the 20th century, was literally possessed by the Holy Spirit. Wigglesworth noted that there is a vast difference between possessing the gift of the Holy Spirit and being possessed by the Holy Spirit. He lived in a realm where he didn't exercise the gifts of the Spirit; the gifts controlled him! He was overtaken by the Spirit so that the Spirit could demonstrate what He wanted to do through any believer who is yielded to such an extent that they become a lightning rod to release the glory."

It is interesting to note that Wigglesworth hadn't gotten his supernatural ministry off the ground until he was over 50 years of age! But when he did get it in full tilt, he managed to raise no fewer than 23 people from the dead!

SHATTERING THE ASCENDANCY OF MATTER

Physicists say that we haven't ever touched matter at all. For example, you actually sit 10 to the -8 meters above a chair and can't even define the positions of the atoms in the chair.

Another example: have you ever tried making two magnets touch at the same polarity? It's next to impossible!

ASTROPHYSICS AND QUANTUM PHYSICS ATTEST TO GOD AS CREATOR. Extra-dimensionality which goes beyond height, width, length and time is borne out by Einstein's Theory of General Relativity and then extended into quantum mechanics' scalar fields and big bang models. Owing to the fact that space-time theorems abound we can deduce that time and space had a beginning and therefore extrapolate the undeniable fact that both time and space are created entities.

WHAT RECENT DISCOVERIES IN ASTROPHYSICS REVEAL ABOUT THE GLORY AND LOVE OF GOD:

"The limits on our abilities to know truth and visualize truth merely remind us that we are the creatures, not the Creator. But the limits do not stop us from seeking to gain a clearer picture of who He is through studying both His inspired Word and His creative work. Each will reveal His glory in its own way. Even if the windows through which we gaze on His realm have a few ripples and dark spots in them, we will be awed at the majestic beauty we see. He has left the curtains open. He invites us to look in."

–David Rogstad, physicist [60]

Jet Propulsion Laboratory

FURTHER ELABORATION ON APPEALING TO HIGHER REALMS - How wonderfully encouraging!

"The tools scientists have used to deal with paradoxes in the physical world can also be applied to gain important insight into various paradoxes in Scriptures. Difficulties that have plagued the Christian community for centuries are not only clarified when 'seen' from the point of view of one living in a higher dimension, but those same difficulties also become the basis for strong proof of the supernatural inspiration of the Bible."

–David Rogstad, physicist [61]

Jet Propulsion Laboratory

PART FOUR: QUANTUM PHYSICS EXPANDING

CHAPTER 12: Expanding our thought and imagination

Our mortal bodies must undergo a BODILY TRANSFORMATION to adapt to another realm as they were only ever intended to perform in a four-dimensional universe with its unique gravity, thermodynamics and electromagnetism.

Now, with an eye on detecting the presence of an extra dimension, let's look directly at some scriptures, comparing the King James Version (KJV) and the New International Version (NIV):

"Now this I say, brethren, that flesh and blood cannot inherit the kingdom of God; neither doth corruption inherit incorruption. [51] Behold, I shew you a mystery; We shall not all sleep, but we shall all be changed, [52] In a moment, in the twinkling of an eye, at the last trump: for the trumpet shall sound, and the dead shall be raised incorruptible, and we shall be changed. [53] For this corruptible must put on incorruption, and this mortal must put on immortality."

1 Corinthians 15:50-53 KJV

An even more scholarly rendition is found in the NEW INTERNATIONAL VERSION:

1 Corinthians 15:50-53 NIV

"I declare to you, brothers and sisters, that flesh and blood cannot inherit the kingdom of God, nor does the perishable inherit the imperishable. [51] Listen, I tell you a mystery: We will not all sleep, but we will all be changed--- [52] in a flash, in the twinkling of an eye, at the last trumpet. For the trumpet will sound, the dead will be raised imperishable, and we will be changed. [53] For the perishable must clothe itself with the imperishable, and the mortal with immortality."

You see, in both translations, we can clearly see that we will still have bodies, or individual identities, to look forward to, but they won't suffer disease, decay or even fatigue, as the laws governing their functionality will dramatically differ from the laws governing ours today. Whatever lies ahead, our new bodies and our new environment will be perfectly in sync.

I WOULD LIKE TO INTRODUCE YOU TO A GROUP OF TWO-DIMENSIONAL BEINGS WHO RESIDE IN MY IMAGINATION. THEY HAVE ONLY LENGTH AND WIDTH, BUT NO HEIGHT.

Can you imagine their flat, two-dimensional bodies trying to live anywhere but on the surface of the computer. Their bodies would simply be too unstable and limited for anything more. We could say the same of our present bodies when we move on to the next dimension. The New English Translation Bible succinctly captures the essence of the moment:

"Dear friends, we are God's children now, and what we will be has not yet been revealed. We know that whenever it is revealed we will be like him, because we will see him just as he is."

1 John 3:2 NET

With an indescribable sight capacity, we will see everything around us in a whole new way, like we've never known before. We will experience life completely new and fresh; all our bodily capacities will be richly enhanced - beyond our wildest imagination!

DO YOU STILL THINK IT'S STRANGE TO PRESUME THAT JUST MAYBE OUR HEAVENLY FATHER RESIDES IN A REALM BEYOND OUR OWN?

God's multi-dimensional advantage can operate in at least eleven dimensions that are borne out by space-time theorems and string theory.

To- B-E-L-I-E-V-E

..

. . . IS

..

ABSOLUTELY

..

EVERYTHING!!

NOT TIMELESSNESS BUT TIME- FULLNESS!!

It's wonderful to know that God is where we're ultimately going and we will hang out with him through all eternity because in fact we're ALREADY THERE! So, when the notion of timelessness becomes part of the deal and begins to sound esoteric, dull and meaningless, we can re-cognize that in God's multi- dimensional realm, we can enjoy glories heretofore unknown.

And we get to do that forever in what we may now wistfully dub "multiple time dimensions".

NOT A GHOST, BUT TANGIBLE AND REAL

"Imagine the disciples' amazement," muses Hugh Ross, "when Jesus came to them bodily, after being crucified, without opening the locked doors or windows of their hideout. Both Luke and John record the event: On the evening of that first day of the week, when the disciples were together, with the doors locked for fear of the Jews, Jesus came and stood among them. . . . They were startled and frightened, thinking they saw a ghost. He said to them, "Why are you troubled, and why do doubts rise in your minds? Look at my hands and my feet. It is I myself! Touch me and see; a ghost does not have flesh and bones, as you see I have." When he had said this, he showed them his hands and feet. And while they still did not believe it because of joy and amazement, he asked them, "Do you have anything here to eat?" They gave him a piece of broiled fish, and he took it and ate it in their presence.19 The disciples' shock arises not only from their inability to comprehend how Jesus could be alive and present but also from their knowledge that physical objects cannot pass through physical barriers without damage to either the object or the barrier. No wonder they concluded that Jesus must be a ghost! What they saw made no sense to them. Jesus responded to their perplexity by demonstrating His physicality. He invited their touch, confirming that He had the solidity of flesh and bones.20 He ate food from their table, further affirming His physical reality.21 The disciples could not know at that moment they had seen an example of what is possible for someone who has access to extra space dimensions or their equivalent."

Dr. Hugh Ross, Ph.D. [62]

Beyond the Cosmos

All things were made by him; and without him was not any thing made that was made.

John 1:3 KJV

For by him were all things created, that are in heaven, and that are in earth, visible and invisible, whether they be thrones, or dominions, or principalities, or powers: all things were created by him, and for him: [17] And he is before all things, and by him all things consist.

Colossians 1:16-17 KJV

CHAPTER 13: Thinking outside the box

MY FORAY into Quantum Physics:

THE DANCING WU LI MASTERS

by Gary Zukav, 1980.

'When I tell my friends that I study physics, they move their heads from side to side, they shake their hands at the wrist, and they whistle, "Whew! That's difficult." This universal reaction to the word "physics" is a wall that stands between what physicists do and what most people think they do. There is usually a big difference between the two. Physicists themselves are partly to blame for this sad situation. Their shop talk sounds like advanced Greek, unless you are Greek or a physicist. When they are not talking to other physicists, physicists speak English. Ask them what they do, however, and they sound like the natives of Corfu again. On the other hand, part of the blame is ours. Generally speaking, we have given up trying to understand what physicists (and biologists, etc.) really do. In this we do ourselves a disservice. These people are engaged in extremely interesting adventures that are not that difficult to understand. True, how they do what they do sometimes entails a technical explanation which, if you are not an expert, can produce an involuntary deep sleep. What physicists do, however, is actually quite simple. They wonder what the universe is really made of, how it works, what we are doing in it, and where it is going, if it is going anyplace at all.'

Dr. Gary Zukav, Ph.D. [63]

The Dancing Wu Li Masters

I'm beginning to think that the insights we're receiving by daring to expand our concepts of the infinitude of God in this way ought to reach mankind more easily. Some of the mind-blowing images that we entertain clear the way for Jesus' miracles to be understood and believed. We don't need to keep bringing limited half-baked constructs to this limited realm but rather point to a dimension beyond what our mortal eyes and brains can grasp. We're not explaining miracles a-w-a-y, we're explaining them to be divinely natural. We're learning that the realm in which God freely lives and moves is closer to us than our very breathing.

It's all about framing dimensions according to laws of physics. For example, the forces of electro-magnetism and gravity afford us a kind of framework for orbits of electrons circling atoms as well as planets circling stars because they follow an inverse square law. Framing can also be done in other dimensions where our standard physics tests no longer apply as we go beyond our human apprehension of statistics.

SPACE AND TIME HAD A BEGINNING. THEREFORE, SPACE AND TIME MUST BE CREATED ENTITIES!

We need only turn to the famous space-time theorem of general relativity to support such a far-reaching claim.

Einstein's Theory of General Relativity shows that there is a singular boundary not just for matter and energy but also for space and time. It describes movements of matter and energy, both the stuff that makes up the universe and the dimensions in which that stuff exists sharing a common origin which translates to a finite beginning.

Therefore, space and time must be created entities, thus laying the groundwork for profound philosophical and theological hypotheses.

APPLICATION:

Meditate on these musings re. FINDING HEALING IN QUANTUM PHYSICS:

*How can matter be in two places at the same time? When you put it through the double slit test, it goes through both or it goes through one and then the other. Also it interacts with what you the Observer are thinking: you can actually get it to do what you want it to do by observing with the right thinking.

*Matter is at once a particle and a wave - that is to say, it flips from one to the other. When it's a particle it can be located since it actually is a piece of matter, i.e., it has mass, albeit, infinitesimal; but when it's a wave, it has no traceable locality.

*Bearing all of that in mind, think about your physical body which you were entirely convinced was made of matter.

*It can also be a wave and in that case it can be entirely healed - owing to its total lack of anything to pin dis-ease on! All that is required is the type of prayer that would take you into another dimension where God resides.

*Imagine impacting something billions of miles away just by thinking about it!

*Imagine impacting something right in front of you just by looking at it!

Quantum mechanics betrays the world's longest held secret – that the universe cannot anywhere near objectively determine its course nor can it ever be entirely free from extraneous measurement.

As wild and esoteric as quantum physics may seem to be, Newtonian (or, general) physics has it beat and has only to be held up to the same non-deterministic testing procedures.

The way that the world actually functions may need to be held to much greater scrutiny, especially in the quantum realm. When new findings are confirmed, it behooves physicists to reevaluate the entire foundation of both general and quantum physics relative to the new discovery until everything 'matches' again.

Gregg Braden [64] admonishes us in his famous masterpiece,

THE DIVINE MATRIX

Bridging time, space, miracles and belief:

"Just as all life is built from the four chemical bases that create our DNA, the universe appears to be founded upon four characteristics of the Divine Matrix that make things work in the way they do. The key to tapping the power of the Matrix lies in our ability to embrace the four landmark discoveries that link it to our lives in an unprecedented way:

Discovery 1: There is a field of energy that connects all of creation.

Discovery 2: This field plays the role of a container, a bridge, and a mirror for the beliefs within us.

Discovery 3: The field is nonlocal and holographic. Every part of it is connected to every other, and each piece mirrors the whole on a smaller scale.

Discovery 4: We communicate with the field through the language of emotion. [REMEMBER THAT RJS DOCTORAL THESIS WHICH OBSERVES EMOTIONAL INVESTMENT IN TOPIC?] It's our power to recognize and apply these realities that determine everything from our healing to the success of our relationships and careers. Ultimately, our survival as a species may be directly linked to our ability and willingness to share life-affirming practices that come from a unified quantum worldview."

CHAPTER 14: Biocentrism

QUANTUM THEORY PROVES CONSCIOUSNESS MOVES TO ANOTHER DIMENSION AFTER DEATH.

Every one of the "miracles" that Jesus effected had everything to do with his having access to other dimensions and availing himself of them as naturally as breathing. He was consciously aware of what he was doing when he raised the dead including himself. So I find it more difficult to believe that suddenly life comes to a screeching halt. And if not, then it goes on; but we don't all see it on this plane of existence. This was my take-away from reading the following treatment of "Biocentrism" by Robert Lanza [65]

Quantum Theory Proves Consciousness Moves To Another Universe After Death

A book titled "Biocentrism: How Life and Consciousness Are the Keys to Understanding the Nature of the Universe" has stirred up the Internet, because it contained a notion that life does not end when the body dies, and it can last forever.

The author of this publication, scientist Dr. Robert Lanza who was voted the 3rd most important scientist alive by the NY Times, has no doubts that this is possible.

1. BEYOND TIME AND SPACE

Lanza is an expert in regenerative medicine and scientific director of Advanced Cell Technology

Company. Before he has been known for his extensive research which dealt with stem cells, he was also famous for several successful experiments on cloning endangered animal species.

But not so long ago, the scientist became involved with physics, quantum mechanics and astrophysics. This explosive mixture has given birth to the new theory of biocentrism, which the professor has been preaching ever since. Biocentrism teaches that life and consciousness are fundamental to the universe. It is consciousness that creates the material universe, not the other way around.

Lanza points to the structure of the universe itself, and that the laws, forces, and constants of the universe appear to be fine-tuned for life, implying intelligence existed prior to matter. He also claims that space and time are not objects or things, but rather tools of our animal understanding. Lanza says that we carry space and time around with us "like turtles with shells." meaning that when the shell comes off (space and time), we still exist.

The theory implies that death of consciousness simply does not exist. It only exists as a thought because people identify themselves with their body. They believe that the body is going to perish, sooner or later, thinking their consciousness will disappear too. If the body generates consciousness, then consciousness dies when the body dies. But if the body receives consciousness in the same way that a cable box receives satellite signals, then of course consciousness does not end at the death of the physical vehicle. In fact, consciousness exists outside of constraints of time and space. It is able to be anywhere: in the human body and outside of it. In other words, it is non-local in the same sense that quantum objects are non-local.

Lanza also believes that multiple universes can exist simultaneously. In one universe, the body can be dead. And in another it continues to exist, absorbing consciousness which migrated into this universe. This means that a dead person while traveling through the same tunnel ends up not in hell or in heaven, but in a similar world he or she once inhabited, but this time alive. And so on, infinitely. It's almost like a cosmic Russian doll afterlife effect.

2. MULTIPLE WORLDS

This hope-instilling, but extremely controversial theory by Lanza has many unwitting supporters, not just mere mortals who want to live forever, but also some well-known scientists. These are the physicists and astrophysicists who tend to agree with existence of parallel worlds and who suggest the possibility of multiple universes. Multiverse (multi-universe) is a so-called scientific concept, which they defend. They believe that no physical laws exist which would prohibit the existence of parallel worlds.

The first one was a science fiction writer H.G. Wells who proclaimed in 1895 in his story "The Door in the Wall". And after 62 years, this idea was developed by Dr. Hugh Everett in his graduate thesis at the Princeton University. It basically posits that at any given moment the universe divides into countless similar instances. And the next moment, these "newborn" universes split in a similar fashion. In some of these worlds you may be present: reading this article in one universe, or watching TV in another.

The triggering factor for these multiplying worlds is our actions, explained Everett. If we make some choices, instantly one universe splits into two with different versions of outcomes.

In the 1980s, Andrei Linde, scientist from the Lebedev's Institute of physics, developed the theory of multiple universes. He is now a professor at Stanford University. Linde explained: Space consists of many inflating spheres, which give rise to similar spheres, and those, in turn, produce spheres in even greater numbers, and so on to infinity. In the universe, they are spaced apart. They are not aware of each other's existence. But they represent parts of the same physical universe.

The fact that our universe is not alone is supported by data received from the Planck space telescope. Using the data, scientists have created the most accurate map of the microwave background, the so-called cosmic relic background radiation, which has remained since the inception of our universe. They also found that the universe has a lot of dark recesses represented by some holes and extensive gaps.

Theoretical physicist Laura Mersini-Houghton from the North Carolina University with her colleagues argue: the anomalies of the microwave background exist due to the fact that our universe is influenced by other universes existing nearby. And holes and gaps are a direct result of attacks on us by neighboring universes.

3. SOUL

So, there is abundance of places or other universes where our soul could migrate after death, according to the theory of neo-biocentrism. But does the soul exist? Is there any scientific theory of consciousness that could accommodate such a claim? According to Dr. Stuart Hameroff, a near-death experience happens when the quantum information that inhabits the nervous system leaves the body and dissipates into the universe. Contrary to materialistic accounts of consciousness, Dr. Hameroff offers an alternative explanation of consciousness that can perhaps appeal to both the rational scientific mind and personal intuitions.

See also: Russian Scientist Photographs Soul Leaving Body And Quantifies Chakras. You Must See This!

Consciousness resides, according to Stuart and British physicist Sir Roger Penrose, in the microtubules of the brain cells, which are the primary sites of quantum processing. Upon death, this information is released from your body, meaning that your consciousness goes with it. They have argued that our experience of consciousness is the result of quantum gravity effects in these microtubules, a theory which they dubbed orchestrated objective reduction (Orch-OR).

Consciousness, or at least proto-consciousness is theorized by them to be a fundamental property of the universe, present even at the first moment of the universe during the Big Bang. "In one such scheme proto-conscious experience is a basic property of physical reality accessible to a quantum process associated with brain activity."

Our souls are in fact constructed from the very fabric of the universe – and may have existed since the beginning of time. Our brains are just receivers and amplifiers for the proto-consciousness that is intrinsic to the fabric of space-time. So is there really a part of your consciousness that is non-material and will live on after the death of your physical body?

Dr Hameroff told the Science Channel's Through the Wormhole documentary: "Let's say the heart stops beating, the blood stops flowing, the microtubules lose their quantum state. The quantum information within the microtubules is not destroyed, it can't be destroyed, it just distributes and dissipates to the universe at large". Robert Lanza would add here that not only does it exist in the universe, it exists perhaps in another universe. If the patient is resuscitated, revived, this quantum information can go back into the microtubules and the patient says "I had a near death experience"

He adds: "If they're not revived, and the patient dies, it's possible that this quantum information can exist outside the body, perhaps indefinitely, as a soul."

This account of quantum consciousness explains things like near-death experiences, astral projection, out of body experiences, and even reincarnation WITHOUT NEEDING TO APPEAL TO RELIGIOUS IDEOLOGY [caps mine]. The energy of your consciousness potentially gets recycled back into a different body at some point, and in the mean time it exists outside of the physical body on some other level of reality, and possibly in another universe.

[I found the above article on Robert Lanza: Biocentrism among my notes and looked high and low for its author, but to no avail.]

The all-caps quote above brings me to one of the key themes of this entire book. "WITHOUT NEEDING TO APPEAL TO RELIGIOUS IDEOLOGY" if referring to all that religious stuff that we have painstakingly and summarily dismissed, is quite noteworthy. By all means, let's avoid bringing religiosity into this picture whatsoever. But God [those two words!] ... if God exists at all - and I most certainly know He does - and if God is omnipotence, omnipresence and omniscience, then I submit to you that everything quantum - from the tiniest atom to the planets in orbit, and beyond, are vibrating in His divinely capable hands.

CHAPTER 15: The "Stuff" we're made of

One single person, imbued with the Spirit, can start a wave of unmitigated exhilaration that effervesces into sheer jubilation at the spectre of discovering ... a whole new world where passion and intellect follow the Holy Spirit's beckoning.

One single fully equipped and alert man or woman of God has it within their power to awaken the entire world to the everywhere presence of God's infinite kingdom where the supernatural and the so-called natural intertwine as One.

YOU ARE A VIBRATIONAL FREQUENCY.

What quantum physics tells us about our origins is staggering. We are all interconnected – even without signals, and experimental evidence is proving our inherent unity, our Non-Locality.

WHAT IS THE PHYSICS OF CONSCIOUSNESS?

With real cutting edge knowledge and the discovery of the "super string field" we find life is basically ONE because unity is at its very foundation. This UNITY is (universal) consciousness, otherwise known as the UNIFIED FIELD and includes absolutely everything: molecules, atoms, quarks, protons, neurons, croutons(!), strings, particles, waves, planets, people, plants, etc. This enlightenment reveals that a wave function is the very stuff that thoughts are made of. The deeper you go into the structure of nature, the less dead matter you'll find: not only is it alive but it's also CONSCIOUS! At its core, the unified field is pure being - intelligence itself. THE SUPER-STRING FIELD (unified field) is exactly what we're made of!!! PURE * ABSTRACT * POTENTIAL * BEING * AWARE * SELF-CONSCIOUSNESS.

"Theoretical Quantum Physicist Dr. Amit Goswami [66] is a retired full professor from the University of Oregon's Department of Physics where he served from 1968 to 1997. He is a pioneer of the new paradigm of science called "science within consciousness," an idea he explicated in his seminal book, The Self-Aware Universe, where he also solved the quantum measurement problem elucidating the famous observer effect.

"Goswami is convinced, along with a number of others who subscribe to the same view, that the universe, in order to exist, requires a conscious sentient being to be aware of it. Without an observer, he claims, it only exists as a possibility. We don't live in a world of electrons or particles. We live in a world of potential electrons and particles that exist in wave-form until the conscious observer comes along and focuses that wave to bring it into existence. The Double-Slit experiment is a perfect example of how consciousness affects the behaviour of quantum objects. Consciousness is the ground of being and underlying fabric of the universe.

Consciousness itself literally gives rise to everything in the universe and the universe can only exist as waves of potential without it, meaning that consciousness itself is more fundamental than material. It is the ground of which the material is a part of. This Unified Field of Intelligence (consciousness) is the Creator of the Universe. "You can call it God if you want, but you don't have to. Quantum consciousness will do."

RJS: HEY, I WANT TO CALL IT GOD BECAUSE THAT'S EXACTLY WHAT GOD IS !!!

"Nonlocality, tangled hierarchy, and discontinuity," Dr. Hagelin continues after my above interruption, "these signatures of quantum consciousness have been independently verified by leading researchers worldwide. This experimental data and its conclusions inform us that it is the mistaken materialist view that is at the center of most of our world's problems today. To address these problems, we now have a science of spirituality that is fully verifiable and objective."

John Hagelin, Ph.D. [67]

From Harvard University

On Consciousness
https://www.youtube.com/watch?v=OrcWntw9juM

Healing and making every aspect of our lives whole again from a baby's sniffles to a permanent love-filled solution to terror attacks at home and abroad, we can join Phil Mason [68] in his celebration of

THE RAW QUANTUM POWER OF GOD:

I have been hit so hard by the raw power of God that I have been knocked to the ground in ecstasy. This has happened far too many times to count.

HOW ABOUT A NEW VIEW OF THE WORLD?

Quantum Entanglement

Quantum dimensions of the Spirit are beautifully articulated by my good friend, Mwanga Leonard Arapsotyo [69] who has greatly inspired me to trust my spiritual revelations and write from the heart:

"The reason He raised you up into the heavenly Places is for you to see things from His perspective. When you know that you are seated with Christ in heavenly places your view of this world will change."

E n T a N g L e M e N t … had always conjured up a highly negative connotation in my life – something I'd want to avoid at all costs. But, as we observe God's precious kingdom unfolding, we know we must revisit this construct with ever greater vigilance.

Can we see God's presence in Gregg Braden's definition of Entanglement as it applies to quantum mechanics? Braden argues,

"Quantum entanglement suggests that once particles are connected, they remain connected on an energetic level, even when they are physically separated from one another. And the really interesting thing is that whether the separation is only a few millimeters or an entire galaxy, the distance doesn't appear to affect the connection. Quantum entanglement exists in the real world, but we can't see it. We can feel it, however, once that filament of connection is forged."

Gregg Braden and Lynn Lauber [70]

ENTANGLEMENT:

A

Tales of Everyday Magic

Novel

I must confess that I am striving – for the life of me – to glean precious knowledge about our uni-verse without losing track of the fact that God – our God – created all of it, connected in a divine entanglement!

******* Another survey! *******

. . . . . APPLICATION . . . . .

HEY, HE SAID IT, NOT ME !!

"The distinction between past, present, and future is only a stubbornly persistent illusion."

-- Albert Einstein [71]

COMMENTS ON EINSTEIN

- Application -

PMF : .. Can you go into your past, not just mentally but physically and can you go into the future?

Robin Starbuck: .. If you're looking for the scientific (physical) answer, you can start a search using the info below. If you're looking for the miraculous, the realm where Jesus healed the sick, raised the dead, walked on water, turned water into wine, fed the multitudes, etc., the answer includes knowing God. Quantum physics straddles the two 'worlds'.

AHS : .. A lil bit of more light on the subject please, Dr.Robin, thanks.

Robin Starbuck : Can you imagine being non-local? Jesus was at times. Always at one with his Father, God, Jesus could place himself wherever he needed to be while Abba, reclining,..."the high and exalted One says—he who lives forever, whose name is holy: "I live in a high and holy place."

Isaiah 57:15 NIV.

While God transcends the temporal realm, the quantum world flips back and forth between our time-ridden existence and that of eternity. Silesius [72], 17th Cent., Pt.1, concludes our conundrum:

.... Do not compute eternity,

.... As light year after year,

.... One step across that line called Time,

.... Eternity is here.

It behooves us, as eager seekers of the truth, to reclaim the entire realm of the quanta, that is, to broadly proclaim that it belongs to God – the Builder and Maker – of the universe! Invisible waves of energy which constitute the quantum field are intimately held in the loving hands of our God, ready to be visited by us as we open our consciousness to His Oneness, Allness and absolute Everywhere-ness! Selah.

G O D , Creator of the universe and beyond, including the quantum world, is here now – within and without.

WHAT DO YOU SOUND LIKE

With the Holy Spirit speaking through you?

What do you see and hear

When God uses your eyes and ears?

And what does it feel like

When Jesus does your feel-ing?

How can you communicate

When God does all the talking?

What then is living like

With God at the very helm?

And what in the world happens

When you run out of questions?

QUESTIONS BEGET QUESTIONS, and new breakthroughs:

Good morning Robin. Have you ever read anything by Gregg Braden [73]? If not, please do. He has a time fractal calculator based in science that determines the time it takes, once a seed (prayer) is sown, for that prayer to manifest into reality. I am fascinated by this because lately I have been declaring things and they happen VERY shortly after. His time fractal calculator (mode 1) shows that when we sow a seed in November 2016 that we shall see the manifestation in December 2016. This resonates with my spirit, and I believe that we will SOON be manifesting things into existence instantaneously just like Jesus. These are exciting times. I shared this with you because I believe that you are one of the few people that could handle this info. This is revelation that may scare some people who are weaker in the faith.

Brian Lawrence [74]

Message

Holding true to Brian Lawrence's high appraisal of Yours Truly's level of spiritual achievement, I am going to make a brazen statement here: God can see into the infinitesimal quantum world just as easily and clearly as He sees all the phenomenon of the macroscopic world, for nothing is hidden from His view. "Nothing in all creation is hidden from God's sight. Everything is uncovered and laid bare before the eyes of Him to whom we must give account." (Hebrews 4:13 NIV) He even knows of every molecule, photon and quark as well as every hair on our collective heads! (Matthew 10:30 NIV)

"As time marches on," Phil Mason [75] prophesies, "new experiments push the frontiers of effective quantum teleportation... The longest distance yet claimed to be achieved for quantum teleportation is 16 kilometers (10 miles) in May 2010 by Chinese scientists over free-space with an average of 89% accuracy." It needs to be pointed out that the days of full scale teleportation of physical objects are still the stuff of science fiction. Up until now quantum teleportation has involved the actual transference of quantum information, but this has certainly paved the way for greater experiments in the future. The success of one experiment lays the foundation for even greater successes."

Permit me, if you will, to repeat Mason's electrifying prediction: "The success of one experiment lays the foundation for even greater successes."

Remember I said earlier that nothing in the universe has ever moved faster than the speed of light? And then they spotted a stray particle doing just that? Blew that theory to smithereens! Hah! That little dot was traveling superluminally! So that knocks the expressions "here" and "there" right outta the quantum entanglement box!

Besides quantum entanglement, quantum tunneling, wave-particle duality, and quantum teleportation all prove matter to be non-local as interactions occur instantaneously no matter how far apart they may be.

NOW, PROSPECTIVE HEALERS, LET'S SEE IF YOU CAN ANSWER ME THIS QUESTION:

If matter is effectively non-local, how in the world does it have the power to manifest as disease?

ANSWER: IT DOES NOT !!!

Let's let Phil Mason further elucidate.

'Physicists have stumbled upon an attribute of the sub-atomic world that compels us to re-think the very nature of the world that we live in. Some eminent thinkers have even speculated that the discovery of the existence of non-local realities would suggest that scientists have accidentally bumped into the reality of the spiritual realm. Other more metaphysically inclined writers would go as far as saying that scientists have discovered "God".'

Phil Mason [76]

Quantum Glory

I, of course, fit in the latter category!

And if you've been thinking that things couldn't get much better than all of this, you'll really find further amazing encouragement in Raymond Chiao's book entitled "The Quantum Wave of Faith." He writes, "The quantum world view of a nonlocal universe has been borne out time and again. Specifically, the Uncertainty Principle has taught us that the classical world view is untenable. Work by Einstein, Bell and many others, including our experiments on quantum tunnelling at Berkeley, have told us that it is impossible to believe in a local, "realistic" universe. This has opened up new possibilities for religious understanding. At the heart of quantum physics is the wave- particle duality. In particular, in the Born interpretation of the wave function, a detection of a particle can be thought of as the materialization of the particle at a particular place at a definite time, out of a wave which is not localized in space nor in time. Although the wave function is itself not directly observable, its properties can be inferred from the manifestations of the particle, which are directly observable."

Raymond Chiao. [77]

The Quantum Wave of Faith.

ON ETERNITY

How often do you ponder the concept of eternity, and for how long? Doesn't it boggle your mind a bit to try to fathom infinity with no time constraints whatsoever?

.... Time is of your own making,

.... Its clock ticks in your head,

.... The moment you stop thought,

.... Time too stops dead.

.... (Silesius [78], 17th cent. Pt.2)

PART FIVE: YOU CAN HEAL YOURSELF NOW

CHAPTER 16: The book starts here!

The purpose of this book is to convince you that you can heal yourself (and, in turn, teach others to heal themselves) as well as give you some solid guidelines. Being in charge of your own healing is the greatest place to be for many reasons and on many levels. For starters, you get to call the shots. But most significantly you are the one who can make your healing stick. You get to learn a great deal about yourself, who is your healer. But, let's get one thing quite clear to avoid any confusion in the future: the real healer is God.

I, personally, have enjoyed so many, many wonderful healings and demonstrations of God's ever-presence and perfect willingness to heal us all. The truth is that after a while, living in the center of God's will becomes a habit that is so secure that you never have to worry about making wrong choices anymore. I haven't totally arrived, but I'm well on my way! It is such a thrill to me to be able to share this with you.

I'm not going to be teaching any secrets or any magic tricks or anything all that unusual except with regard to degree. People just have no idea how very close they come to a complete healing but they don't hang in there long enough or strong enough. They don't go deep enough or far enough or high enough. What I really mean is they don't believe the very truth that they are applying and so the healing simply peters out.

DOES THE BIBLE UNAMBIGUOUSLY SUPPORT HEALING?

100+ biblical references to healing:

Old Testament

1) I am the Lord that healeth thee (Ex. 15:26).

2) Your days shall be one hundred and twenty years (Gen. 6:3).

3) You shall be buried in a good old age (Gen. 15:15).

4) You shall come to your grave in a full age like as a shock of corn cometh in his season (Job 5:26).

5) When I see the blood, I will pass over you and the plague shall not be upon you to destroy you (Ex. 12:13).

6) I will take sickness away from the midst of you and the number of your days I will fulfill (Ex. 23: 25, 26).

7) I will not put any of the diseases you are afraid of on you, but I will take all sickness away from you (Deut. 7:15).

8) It will be well with you and your days shall be multiplied and prolonged as the days of heaven upon the earth (Deut. 11:9,21).

9) I turned the curse into a blessing unto you, because I loved you (Deut. 23:5 and Neh. 13:2).

10) I have redeemed you from every sickness and every plague (Deut. 28:61 and Gal. 3:13).

11) As your days, so shall your strength be (Deut. 33:25).

12) I have found a ransom for you, your flesh shall be fresher than a child's and you shall return to the days of your youth (Job 33:24, 25).

13) I have healed you and brought up your soul from the grave; I have kept you alive from going down into the pit (Ps. 30:1, 2).

14) I will give you strength and bless you with peace (Ps. 29:11).

15) I will preserve you and keep you alive (Ps. 41:2).

16) I will strengthen you upon the bed of languishing; I will turn all your bed in your sickness (Ps. 41:3).

17) I am the health of your countenance and your God (Ps.43: 5).

18) No plague shall come near your dwelling (Ps. 91:10).

19) I will satisfy you with long life (Ps. 91:16).

20) I heal all your diseases (Ps. 103:3).

21) I sent My word and healed you and delivered you from your destructions (Ps. 107:20).

22) You shall not die, but live, and declare My works (Ps. 118:17).

23) I heal your broken heart and bind up your wounds (Ps. 147:3).

24) The years of your life shall be many (Pr. 4:10).

25) Trusting Me brings health to your navel and marrow to your bones (Pr. 3:8).

26) My words are life to you, and health/medicine to all your flesh (Pr. 4:22).

27) (My) good report makes your bones fat (Pr. 15:30).

28) (My) pleasant words are sweet to your soul and health to your bones (Pr. 16:24).

29) My joy is your strength. A merry heart does good like a medicine (Neh. 8:10; Pr. 17:22).

30) The eyes of the blind shall be opened. The eyes of them that see shall not be dim (Isa. 32:3; 35:5).

31) The ears of the deaf shall be unstopped. The ears of them that hear shall hearken (Isa. 32:3; 35:5).

32) The tongue of the dumb shall sing. The tongue of the stammerers shall be ready to speak plainly (Isa. 35:6; 32:4).

33) The lame man shall leap as a hart (Isa. 35:6).

34) I will recover you and make you to live. I am ready to save you (Isa. 38:16, 20).

35) I give power to the faint. I increase strength to them that have no might (Isa. 40:29).

36) I will renew your strength. I will strengthen and help you (Isa. 40:31; 41:10).

37) To your old age and gray hairs I will carry you and I will deliver you (Isa. 46:4).

38) I bore your sickness (Isa. 53:4).

39) I carried your pains (Isa. 53:4).

40) I was put to sickness for you (Isa. 53:10).

41) With My stripes you are healed (Isa. 53:5).

42) I will heal you (Isa. 57:19).

43) Your light shall break forth as the morning and your health shall spring forth speedily (Isa. 58:8).

44) I will restore health unto you, and I will heal you of your wounds saith the Lord (Jer. 30:17).

45) Behold I will bring it health and cure, and I will cure you, and will reveal unto you the abundance of peace and truth (Jer. 33:6).

46) I will bind up that which was broken and will strengthen that which was sick (Eze. 34:16).

47) Behold, I will cause breath to enter into you and you shall live. And I shall put My Spirit in you and you shall live (Eze. 37:5,14).

48) Whithersoever the rivers shall come shall live. They shall be healed and every thing shall live where the river comes (Eze. 47:9).

49) Seek Me and you shall live (Amos 5:4, 6).

50) I have arisen with healing in My wings (beams) (Mal. 4:2).

New Testament

51) I will, be thou clean (Mt. 8:3).

52) I took your infirmities (Mt. 8:17).

53) I bore your sicknesses (Mt. 8:17).

54) If you're sick you need a physician. (I am the Lord your physician) (Mt. 9:12 & Ex. 15:26).

55) I am moved with compassion toward the sick and I heal them (Mt. 14:14).

56) I heal all manner of sickness and all manner of disease (Mt. 4:23).

57) According to your faith, be it unto you (Mt. 9:29).

58) I give you power and authority over all unclean spirits to cast them out, and to heal all manner of sickness and all manner of disease (Mt. 10:1 & Lk. 9:1).

162

59) I heal them all (Mt. 12:15 & Heb. 13:8).

60) As many as touch Me are made perfectly whole (Mt. 14:36).

61) Healing is the children's bread (Mt. 15:26).

62) I do all things well. I make the deaf to hear and the dumb to speak (Mk. 7:37).

63) If you can believe, all things are possible to him that believeth (Mk. 9:23; 11:23, 24).

64) When hands are laid on you, you shall recover (Mk. 16:18).

65) My anointing heals the brokenhearted, and delivers the captives, recovers sight to the blind, and sets at liberty those that are bruised (Lk. 4:18; Isa. 10:27; 61:1).

66) I heal all those who have need of healing (Lk. 9:11).

67) I am not come to destroy men's lives but to save them (Lk. 9:56).

68) Behold, I give you authority over all the enemy's power and nothing shall by any means hurt you (Lk. 10:19).

69) Sickness is satanic bondage and you ought to be loosed today (Lk. 13:16 & II Cor. 6:2).

70) In Me is life (Jn. 1:4).

71) I am the bread of life. I give you life (Jn. 6:33, 35).

72) The words I speak unto you are spirit and life (Jn. 6:63).

73) I am come that you might have life, and that you might have it more abundantly (Jn. 10:10).

74) I am the resurrection and the life (Jn. 11:25).

75) If you ask anything in My name, I will do it (Jn. 14:14).

76) Faith in My name makes you strong and gives you perfect soundness (Acts 3:16).

77) I stretch forth My hand to heal (Acts 4:30).

78) I, Jesus Christ, make you whole (Acts 9:34).

79) I do good and heal all that are oppressed of the devil (Acts 10:38).

80) My power causes diseases to depart from you (Acts 19:12).

81) The law of the Spirit of life in Me has made you free from the law of sin and death (Rom. 8:2).

82) The same Spirit that raised Me from the dead now lives in you and that Spirit will quicken your mortal body (Rom. 8:11).

83) Your body is a member of Me (I Cor. 6:15).

84) Your body is the temple of My Spirit and you're to glorify Me in your body (I Cor. 6:19, 20).

85) If you'll rightly discern My body which was broken for you, and judge yourself, you'll not be judged and you'll not be weak, sickly or die prematurely (I Cor. 11:29-31).

86) I have set gifts of healing in My body (I Cor. 12:9).

87) My life may be made manifest in your mortal flesh (II Cor. 4:10, 11).

88) I have delivered you from death, I do deliver you, and if you trust Me I will yet deliver you (II Cor. 1:10).

89) I have given you My name and have put all things under your feet (Eph. 1:21, 22).

90) I want it to be well with you and I want you to live long on the earth. (Eph. 6:3).

91) I have delivered you from the authority of darkness (Col. 1:13).

92) I will deliver you from every evil work (II Tim. 4:18).

93) I tasted death for you. I destroyed the devil who had the power of death. I've delivered you from the fear of death and bondage (Heb. 2:9, 14,15).

94) I wash your body with pure water (Heb. 10:22; Eph. 5:26).

95) Lift up the weak hands and the feeble knees. Don't let that which is lame be turned aside but rather let Me heal it (Heb. 12:12, 13).

96) Let the elders anoint you and pray for you in My name and I will raise you up (Jas. 5:14, 15).

97) Pray for one another and I will heal you (Jas. 5:16).

98) By My stripes you were healed (I Pet. 2:24).

99) My Divine power has given unto you all things that pertain unto life and godliness through the knowledge of Me (II Pet. 1:3).

100) And whosoever will, let him take the water of life freely. (Rev. 22:7)

101) Beloved, I wish above all things that thou mayest..be in health (III John 2)

The Bible: King James Version (KJV).

…

If you have any issue in your life that is in need of healing – probably because all standard measures failed – and you'd like God to help you, you've come to the right place. But you've also heard of failures and disappointments due to trusting religion, right? Well, take heart …. I HATE ORGANIZED RELIGION TOO !! . There, I said it. (Please see Part I, Chapters 1-4) for a more thorough treatment of this critical fact. Then come back here and we'll continue.)

There is a need to "bind the strong man" (the false belief that the body has a mind of its own and can dictate its terms and conditions). It was Jesus who posed the rhetorical question: "How can one enter into a strong man's house and spoil his goods, except he first bind the strong man?" Of course, He didn't need to deal with sickness on a step-by-step basis as He saw through the presentations of the flesh. Such questions like the above were for our benefit! Destroy dis-ease in the mind, including and especially its fear aspect, and you have ridden your patient (yourself) of the disease.

The best place for us to start is at the beginning with a conversation with God. Let Him know that your goal has already begun to shift a bit. You're starting to focus on who and what He is and why He loves you so much. Well, He created you out of His very own substance, so what's not to love? He is present everywhere in this realm and way, way beyond. And He's your intimate friend as well as Creator.

Are you still saying you want to see results? Or, have you already grown in grace enough to realize that your shift, albeit miniscule, is a huge step forward. The Holy Spirit tells us "I am in you and ALL around you. I'm in your mind and every cell of your body. My thinking is your thinking and you're My very be-ing. I love you passionately and know you love Me as well. Remember, though, that every single person who comes to your mind – I love them too, with respect and awe. You want to know what's special about you? It's your own unique awareness."

There are far too many arguments flying around out there which damn and criticize other people's prayer methodologies when a much more effective and efficient stance to assume is "Hey, whatever works!" The bottom line is that the patient (yourself, for example) needs to be awakened.

Awakened, that is, to the antipode of what he has been clinging to! God is right here, now, instead of the pain, poverty, disability or disillusionment. I know you think you can't see that now, but you can. Flood your precious God-given mind with images of Him and His love. Do not allow yourself to drift into that former place where you felt trapped and hopeless.

I need to tell you what I'm about to try to prepare you for. With the right preparation and a whole lot of trust, you will become receptive to a healing realm that is astronomical! You'll be able to count on it anytime, anyplace, anywhere!

When I said "flood your mind with..." I should have said "Open your mind to God alone and let HIM flood it for you!" He loves to do that because, as you know, He IS Love and He loves you.

And, because it's true that our bodies are divinely designed to heal themselves, we can feel very much encouraged to pray accordingly – and expect great results – even if we've been confined to a wheelchair for 20+ years, have the flu, cancer, aids, poverty, etc., there is healing in God.

We need to be aware that this healing power is within us. Let's understand that, while there is nothing we can or should do to get God's attention and beg for favor, there is a great deal that we can and should do to align our own thinking with the Mind of God.

EVERY TIME YOU TURN OFF THE WORLD in your mind and just listen to God speaking to you directly from the inside – every time you keep listening no matter what the distractions, every time you turn your back on the slightest interruption and listen to Him with your whole heart, soul, mind, He will tell you great and wonderful things specifically for you in your life.

He's saying to you right now: "May I begin by saying let's call it Our life – the life that you and I share as one being and the reason that I am always with you. I love you; I have always loved you and I always will. We have great and wonderful things to do together as One person."

We can begin by recognizing that our vision is perfect and we can "see" our every-brother as he was created: pure and perfect, like us. We can hear with the same measure of perfection that God gave us from before the beginning of time: we can demonstrate it here and now. We are healed and whole, just as we were always intended to be.

"... [W]e know that if one soul ever heard from Heaven, another soul may. If one soul ever had an interview with God, another soul may. If any man ever knew his sins were forgiven at any period, another man may know his sins are forgiven now. If a man or woman ever was healed by the power of God, then men and women can be healed again. The only thing necessary is to return again in soul experience to that same place of intimacy where the first individual met God."

John G. Lake [79]

(a great healer)

When you're ready to test out this new relationship you've just come into, you'll enjoy lots and lots of smaller demonstrations of God's willingness to love on you in wonderful, highly personal ways. For example, one day I was feeling this thing called 'meh', coupled with a little symptomatic stuff, kinda yukky. I began to wonder how to get instantaneous healing, regeneration and joy, when PAPA (Abba, God) said "Breathe!" I replied that I was planning to anyway. He said "hehehe, now breathe!" I took in a nice l-o-o-o-ng breath (just one) and I felt love and joy and excitement and healing – all rushing in and utterly replacing the former junk.

There was no prayer of petition, no asking, no nothing. I just listened and there it was!!!

CHAPTER 17: Okay, now here's the part that I've been preparing you for!

Neville Goddard [80], in 'Anything You Want' offers us this amazing counsel:

"[W]hat is real and what is imaginary when, in a spiritual sense, all existing things are imaginary? Mark tells the parable of the fig tree, which – having been cursed – was found withered to its roots. Calling attention to this fact, awakened imagination said: "Have faith in God. Truly I say to you, whoever says to this mountain, 'Be taken up and cast into the sea,' and does not doubt in his heart that what he has said will come to pass, it will be done for him. Therefore I tell you, whatever you desire, when you pray believe you have received it and you will." Mark 11.

"Here is an imaginary act which has no support in fact. The tree was not withered at the time it was cursed, but when they returned the next day the imaginal act had been executed. So you see: this law is not limited to being constructive only. It can be used for good, bad, or indifferent purposes; for there are no limitations placed on the possibilities of prayer. Now when you pray you must immerse yourself in the feeling of the wish fulfilled, for the word "pray" means, "Motion towards; accession to; at or in the vicinity of." Point yourself towards the wish fulfilled and accept that invisible state as reality. Then go your way knowing the desire is now yours. You did it and you will not be surprised when it comes to pass. When you first practice this technique you will be surprised when it happens; but when you learn how to completely accept the state assumed, you will know you do not have to do a thing to make it come to pass, as the assumption contains its own plan of fulfillment. You will know that this world is imaginal and that an assumption – with no external object to support its truth – will harden into fact when its truth is persisted in."

Anything we want can be ours - that's quite a statement! All we have to do is to immerse ourselves in the feeling of the wish fulfilled! It's got to be a taller order than meets the eye, doesn't it? Yes, indeed, unless we expand our ability to see beyond the limitations of the flesh. To this end we have a willing friend in Quantum Physics, discussed in Part III and Part IV.

It is one thing to have one's prayers answered with exacting regularity and in ways that exceed our wildest expectations but quite another thing to simply function at a level of perfect oneness with the Creator of the universe – and beyond – in the sweetest, most intimate relationship imaginable! If you think this is too far-fetched to admit of reality, think again!

Would you try a little experiment with me right now, please? Think back to the last time you were so happy that you thought you'd explode with a superabundance of indescribable joy. Okay, now that's what we're reaching for – to establish on a permanent basis. Okay? (The healing thing is just a small part of the whole package!)

I'D LIKE TO SHARE SOMETHING INTIMATE WITH YOU: I want to earn your trust in my integrity with a little self-intro and a social media encounter that occurred almost five years ago.

There's something burning so strongly within me that it feels like it could explode at any time. I know that a deeply intimate relationship with God can be had by every single individual on the planet and I also know that, for the most part, this is not happening! Big deal, you say? You're missing my point.

WHO DOESN'T KNOW SOMEONE IN NEED OF HEALING?

If you're fumbling now with all due skepticism, you're just the person I want to talk to. You've seen quacks and you've heard half-baked accounts of people putting all their trust in some method or person or book or psycho-theological theory. I am none of these. I don't want any money, any following, any notoriety or fame. I JUST WANT TO GIVE YOU THIS MESSAGE FROM GOD: You can be healed and you can teach others to heal themselves as well.

I began to share some principles on how this is done when one person cut me to the quick nearly 5 years ago. She was in so much heartache and pain over her husband's passing from cancer that she could only hear

EVERYTHING THAT I WAS NOT SAYING. I wanted to tell her so many things, but she took every single thing I said wrong as if any present discovery would be nothing more than an ongoing punishment for her. She couldn't, for the life of her, stop focusing on the past and stop blaming people in the present who want to teach people - especially the young - that there is a loving God, very much available to them. We parted ways with no miraculous resolution. Not, unless her story can be helpful to us now.

THE SADDEST THING THAT PEOPLE AUTOMATICALLY DO with regard to 'new' revelation on the topic of spiritual healing is to jump back into some prior knowledge or experience and mercilessly stir it all up into one big mess of skepticism, doubt, fear, ridicule and apathy. IF THERE IS ANYTHING OF ANY VALUE TO BE SHARED, it can't be received in such an impure atmosphere. One must suspend judgement and really, really try not to delve into the past at all. I couldn't bring back her dead husband of yesteryear and she wasn't ready to hear anything about connecting with God in order to LET HIM BECOME HER ONLY TEACHER AND GUIDE. She bought into human psychology's dictum that she needed an interminable period of time to grieve.

I have no formula to offer, no pat answers, no soothing words. But I do know that:

The truth can't make you free

UNLESS you 'know' the truth!

John 8:32 KJV

And ye shall know the truth, and the truth shall make you free.

...

Can you

Impersonalize

Evil?

Can you

Nothingize

Evil?

My thoughts about those questions are: Yes and yes. I can APPLY the truth that if God didn't create it, it isn't created. How do I APPLY it? Simply by recognizing/ knowing the truth that is the replacement for the lie. Furthermore, I believe that anyone can effect miracles.

Oh sure, you could argue that it's not you that brings them about, but I would say they needed you to "see" them, to believe God for them. We, too, need to rise to that consciousness (that realm) where miracles take place; and to do so we must transcend the human consciousness, remembering that it's "not that we are sufficient of ourselves to think any thing as of ourselves; but our sufficiency is of God (2 Corinthians 3:5 KJV)."

Do you tend to see pairs of opposites everywhere in life? That's the first thing that needs to go! There are not two powers - good and evil, mortal and immortal, God and the devil. There is but one power, one presence, one reality and ALL YOU HAVE TO DO IS SEE IT !!!

All power inheres in God. Period.

...

GIVE UP

Your belief in

Two Powers!

...

PERSONAL EQUIPPING

I do not belong to myself

Anymore.

It's over with all that!

Been so for many years now

Despite any seeming.

Many, many years ago

After years and years of joyful serving,

I said, "What, now, Lord?"

He paused for 3 or 4 long seconds

And said, "How about we get you a Ph.D.?"

What? Me? Why? In what? Where? When? How? Me???

"Some people, like you,

Have been so badly beaten down

For so long, by so many

And yet they persist in staying alive

They need to be heard. That's why."

Said God.

To me.

...

CHAPTER 18: Typical call for healing

One rather frustrated inquirer wrote:

"I personally dont have a grasp of this healing stuff. I know it is real based on the Scriptures, "the prayer of a righteous person avails much" and "by his stripes we are healed". and seen answered prayers and usually they are sudden, not some ritual/ procedure..drawn out over time, yet don't understand why personally I have not been healed of some chronic pain problems that keep me from almost walking some days from numerous accidents, injuries that have wreaked havoc speedily over past 5 years or so. Now at first I thought I needed to find a bro or sis that had the spiritual gift of healing, yet you listen to [a healer] and he says it always doesn't work that way. Then you hear it's your faith, then your faith has nothing to do with it. Then it's not God will. then it's God's will to heal..to the point that it's like making up excuses for God not healing ...really sucks because if it possible, I need it and want it..or I can make up that which borderlines as an excuse for it not happening to remind me of the many, many times God has snatched me up from death in accidents but God doesn't need me making excuses for Him, He either heals or does not...just not understanding area and want some definate answers." C.J.H.

Response:

You'll want to line up your thinking with God-mindedness because you need to make yourself receptive to your own unique 'answer'. If your thinking were 51% receptive to God's input, you would have more on the side of victory than defeat. Keep reading....

A VERY SICK PERSON, IN DESPERATION, seeks healing in Christ. He is told:

"You are the very image and likeness of your Creator. God lives within you, through you, and as you. All that God is, you are. 'As He is, so are you in this world.' You cannot possibly be sick unless you choose to accept instead a false (albeit universal) belief. If you choose the latter then you need to get it under control. You can read it the riot act; you can do your level best to bind it; you can call people to get together and hold a vigil over it, protesting its weakness, impotence, and disgusting dastardliness. Or you could treat "IT" according to the first choice, namely, that it is a false belief, and simply dismiss it.

Okay now, dear reader, I have YOU in mind. That's right, You. I hear You saying, "Robin, I'm being patient, but I don't 'see' anything happening. You're telling me everything's already done and I don't have to do anything. But you're also telling me that I've gotta adjust my thinking so that I can open up an awareness of a whole new way of thinking. That doesn't seem like nothing to me!"

Robin's response: YOUR question is very, very helpful. The fact that you started it off by bringing up the importance of being able to 'see' the answer is very telling. That is EXACTLY my point. You don't need to DO anything to make the perfection of God true, and you don't need to DO anything to get Him on the inside of you. He lives there. But you could spend an entire lifetime unaware that He's there, that He loves you and that He wants to fellowship with you. So, if you have been filling that precious mind and heart of yours with so much junk which flatly denies God's all-power and ever-presence day after day, year after year, it will take a bit of convincing to BRING YOU TO THE POINT WHERE YOU THOUGHT YOU ALREADY WERE, namely, wanting spiritual healing to bear on your physical condition. You are right in assuming that you need to 'see' this.

Now, I didn't exactly say that you have to adjust your thinking - that could be a job of astronomical proportions! No, we only need to focus on God, and He will do the rest. The more that you realize how cool He really is, the more clearly you'll see Him on the inside of you. You'll start to hear Him too - not in an audible voice, usually, but in the gentlest, most loving inner sound or feeling imaginable. You'll feel the most wonderful change taking place inside and out, and this is the REAL CLINCHER: so many glorious things will start coming into your life that you will literally FORGET your original complaint. Somewhere along the way it will be replaced by total healing - INCLUDING THE NECESSARY ADJUSTMENTS IN YOUR ENVIRONMENT to sustain it.

So, remember, it doesn't really do any good to speak aloud what you want if you haven't ever put any faith in God's words. You've got to have the Word of God take over in your consciousness. Let His Word recreate you, as it were, so that His perfection can take over your entire being. When you let God take charge of your very feelings, that's when everything changes and your life starts to measure up to the divine. You won't want things that could pull you back down anymore because the desire to have things that were designed to throw you off your course . . . you'll simply see through them and have a little chuckle. You'll want more and more of God and you'll have more and more of God almost simultaneously! And, oh yes, it will be thrilling! You just have no idea how much power you wield from the inside of you - it is mind-boggling! So much junk will fall by the wayside and you will speak with authority, dignity and power.

The very next step is to remove the word "will" from everything above (and below). We're talking about a here and now hands on reality!! Take Mark 11:23 for example and speak to your mountain - but do not turn to the fleshly mind to choose something to test it with. Your prayers must line up with the obvious will of God. At this moment I'm sure you can't imagine how reassuring it is to know that you must align yourself with God's will and that God's will is very obvious and clear. As a matter of fact if you would give all prideful considerations over to God right now - every last one of them - you'll suddenly feel infinitely lighter and you'll realize that you are on the King's Highway right now!!

Faith in your own words is going to burst forth like a wellspring of water set free! It will all be so compelling to you! First and foremost, turn to your Bible and let the Word of God in. Its impact must reign and rule in your heart: your desires will undergo a metamorphosis as you trust the Bible to feed you and re--form you. It will be more thrilling than your first kiss! Your first kiss won't even be able to hold a candle to what you will experience when you truly, truly listen to the Holy Spirit who resides on the inside of you! The righteousness of your own prayers will dazzle you and the immediacy of the Word will utterly disarm you of all else.

Did you really wonder where you got that supernatural confidence and supernatural faith from? Really? You didn't know? That's you! That's the real you! That's the God-within-you You! I wonder if you will drop all else and let the Word of God direct you in -e-v-e-r-y-t-h-i-n-g-.

"The law of the Lord is perfect, converting the soul: the testimony of the Lord is sure, making wise the simple. [8] The statutes of the Lord are right, rejoicing the heart: the commandment of the Lord is pure, enlightening the eyes. [9] The fear of the Lord is clean, enduring for ever: the judgments of the Lord are true and righteous altogether. [10] More to be desired are they than gold, yea, than much fine gold: sweeter also than honey and the honeycomb. [14] Let the words of my mouth, and the meditation of my heart, be acceptable in thy sight, O Lord, my strength, and my redeemer."

Psalm 19:7-10, 14 KJV

That's the beginning of your healing: exchanging disease-producing thoughts for glorious healing ones!

WHERE HEALING IS FOUND

I ran into a friend the other day. There was no collateral damage, lol. I started this article with a spot of levity as a contrast to the deeply serious topic I want to discuss: UNHEALED BODIES & UNANSWERED PRAYERS.

I just took a deep gulp and asked God if we must write about this, to which He responded, "Oh yes, there are some who need it." So, here it is:

* To bake a cake, you've got to collect the right ingredients and put the correct amounts in, in the right order, stir appropriately and cook for the right amount of time. Otherwise you'll encounter failure. Even a man can follow these simple instructions, if he wants to!

* My friend, whom I alluded to above, unloaded his life's concerns on me, and they were pretty scary. He carries a lot of anger and sadness around wherever he goes. He prays, he praises the Lord and he reads his Good Book. He's glad he has a nice job but feels the boss should be tarred and feathered. His marriage is okay but his wife is a big problem (his words were more colorful). And he can't understand why Jesus won't heal his long-standing illness. He goes to church and he's even reading a book about more effective praying. He's at the end of his rope and fit to be tied!

CHAPTER 19: Where healing is

If you have any reason to believe that God heals - any reason whatsoever - THEN the next step is to get the mind and heart tuned in to the realm of God - where healing resides. (Think of it as the REALm of the REAL.) Success is in direct proportion to our getting there and -s-t-a-y-i-n-g- there. I've heard of people jumping through the hoops, doing everything humanly possible to secure a healing, and none came. There's so much wrong with this approach that I don't know where to begin. It's entirely relegated to the human, material dimension. Jesus' supernatural healings and miracles were not. God needs to be understood aright in order to access his all-power, all-knowing, all-presence.

AN EXPERIMENT IN GOD

I am going to type a little squiggle. Please take a look at it:

¿°》

NOW THE IMPORTANT QUESTION IS NOT "WHAT" YOU SAW –

THE IMPORTANT QUESTION FOR YOU TO ANSWER IS "HOW" YOU SAW IT.

"I just looked at it."

"I saw it with my eyes."

"You told me to look at it."

"How could I have missed it?"

"With my eyes, silly!"

"It was right there."

"This is stupid."

"I couldn't miss it..."

"I opened my eyes and looked."

This is how it is with God within you. What do you have to do to activate the power? Nothing. Look, or, don't look – it's right there. In you.

You don't need to petition God. You don't need to do anything IN ORDER TO REALIZE THAT GOD IS IN YOU.

When a person

Faces a challenge

Big or small

By trusting God

All the way

He's not surprised

To receive

A perfect answer.

His faith begins

To soar

His confidence too.

Next time

He trusts again

And again and again.

He becomes filled

With a kind of

God confidence

And no longer needs

To prove himself

When, in fact,

all that there is

Is God.

Sometimes we unwittingly harbor an interest in staying sick - at least in some aspects of our life. Unbeknownst to us, we are still holding someone responsible for our misfortune or illness. That person may have been dead for 10 years already - even more - but we don't want to let go because playing the victim is more titillating, albeit very, very costly, to our complete and permanent healing.

What if God were all that you had, nothing else? What if your every thought and desire were to simply peter out … and there were nothing … whatsoever … left … but you … and God?

People spend way too much time analyzing various approaches to healing and then conduct their lives superficially. They try this method and that method but they NEVER QUITE GO DEEPLY ENOUGH!

When one half-hearted attempt doesn't bring instantaneous results, they believe they've disproven the method and they wander off. They never come anywhere near reaching their goal because they never reach for it strongly enough. They weep and wail and swoon and croon – but it never takes them far enough out of their hypnotic, sickly state. This can come to an end right now as we use the greatest mind-expanding ploy imaginable: plunging into the depths of Quantum physics. This is tantamount to magnifying reality itself exponentially! We can sail past our little lives to the extent that the cares and woes literally CEASE TO EXIST.

So, basically we need to get you thinking outside the box. Deeper, farther, higher, longer, bigger; and in the case of quantum mechanics, we'll even go tinier – into the far reaches of an atom. But let's do a little more expanding in our day-to-day thinking and living first. We can plunge fully into subatomic particles as soon as we deal with a few more particles here on terra firma.

Let's prepare our mind by bringing up the issue of Who our Healer is that we are endeavoring to reach beyond the cosmos to contact for the dearest, most intimate relationship known to mankind.

HELP YOUR HEALING

Step away from the pain.

You CAN do so.

Head high, shoulders back.

Don't LOOK for trouble

In your body.

Feel the perfection

Everywhere and rejoice!

Someone loves you

And wants you just as

He created you to be.

Now, don't go back

To the former pain.

Go forever out, into the light,

Into your eternal

Sabbath rest.

The Right Answers

When we find ourselves involved in a controversial topic of some importance, we need to make sure that we are representing the One Who will make the entire undertaking a divinely productive one: after all we're dealing with things of the spirit, n'est pas? For example, I am a firm believer in the fact that God's work is completely done, so it would be futile for me to beg him to have mercy on me and send me his favor when it's already been done. And yet, I have no qualms about praying the prayer of desperation when I need an immediate answer: "God, help!" Suddenly the way tends to open up and answers tend to flood in.

WE'RE DEALING WITH THINGS OF THE SPIRIT

Our anointed nature must surely kick in and fully equip us to address such seemingly contradictory issues as:

(A) Doesn't God want one thing and one thing only: that we believe on him?

(B) What about the billions of people who are not capable of knowing God, due to geography, religion, education, financial status?

We absolutely must turn to the mind of God to reveal to us what He wants us to know. I know the human answers to both questions but now I want to know what God has implanted in my heart that I haven't been able to pull up yet.

"God, please help!"

is a good prayer

A quick fix, or

For an emergency.

It never fails, but

Has a limited scope.

"God, please help"

Implies that He

Should assist us

In our little lives.

I've used it often,

I confess, but now

It's not so much that

I want or need Him

To help me with

My little plan(s)

But more that

I quit all that, and

Just want to know

What We —

Him and me

Will do now and

Always, as ONE!!

CHAPTER 20: Immediacy

Wouldn't you like to apply Bible verses and promises to take place here and now in your life according to Jesus' own words "IT IS FINISHED"? . Open your Bible - for example - to Ephesians 1:1 and start reading. Remember, God's part is done. We want to access His finished work. After all, He's living on the inside of us, right? When did you want to receive your answers? A week from next Monday? Then close your Bible and wait till then! [Sorry, I digressed.] Back to Ephesians - down to 17:

(Ephesians 1:17-23 KJV)

That the God of our Lord Jesus Christ, the Father of glory, may give unto you the spirit of wisdom and revelation in the knowledge of him: [18] The eyes of your understanding being enlightened; that ye may know what is the hope of his calling, and what the riches of the glory of his inheritance in the saints, [19] And what is the exceeding greatness of his power to us-ward who believe, according to the working of his mighty power, [20] Which he wrought in Christ, when he raised him from the dead, and set him at his own right hand in the heavenly places , [21] Far above all principality, and power, and might, and dominion, and every name that is named, not only in this world, but also in that which is to come: [22] And hath put all things under his feet, and gave him to be the head over all things to the church, [23] Which is his body, the fulness of him that filleth all in all.

And now we extrapolate from our reading to give ourselves a powerful affirmation, like this:

ALL THAT POWER AND STRENGTH AND WISDOM AND LOVE IS MINE N-O-W LIVING ON THE INSIDE OF ME. MY POWER FAR EXCEEDS ALL PRINCIPALITIES AND RULERS OF DARKNESS. I AM HEALED RIGHT NOW. GOD IS HERE INSTEAD OF THE (YOU NAME IT – IT'S GONE!!) . GET UP, SHAKE OFF THE HYPNOTIC HOLD IT HAD OVER YOU. IT'S GONE. KEEP READING. KEEP APPLYING. NOT FOR SOME TIME IN THE FUTURE – EVEN TEN MINUTES FROM NOW. GOD'S BLESSINGS ARE NOT ON THEIR WAY – THEY'RE HERE NOW WITHIN YOU!! . DON'T GO BACK TO THE LIE. DON'T TALK ABOUT WHAT THE DIS-EASE HAS BEEN SHOWING YOU – ITS SHOWING DAYS ARE OVER!!

Continuing to read Paul's words, I have to choke back tears of thankfulness for his example of being completely given over to God as I yearn to be.

Ephesians 3:7-14, 18-19 KJV

Whereof I was made a minister, according to the gift of the grace of God given unto me by the effectual working of his power. [8] Unto me, who am less than the least of all saints, is this grace given, that I should preach among the Gentiles the unsearchable riches of Christ; [9] And to make all men see what is the fellowship of the mystery, which from the beginning of the world hath been hid in God, who created all things by Jesus Christ: [10] To the intent that now unto the principalities and powers in heavenly places might be known by the church the manifold wisdom of God, [11] According to the eternal purpose which he purposed in Christ Jesus our Lord: [12] In whom we have boldness and access with confidence by the faith of him. [13] Wherefore I desire that ye faint not at my tribulations for you, which is your glory. [14] For this cause I bow my knees unto the Father of our Lord Jesus Christ, [18] May be able to comprehend with all saints what is the breadth, and length, and depth, and height; [19] And to know the love of Christ, which passeth knowledge, that ye might be filled with all the fulness of God.

PAUL DIDN'T THINK ABOUT, MEDITATE ON, TALK ABOUT OR DISPLAY HIS OWN BODY: HIS FOCUS WAS SINGLE. The Lord was his love and his life. He gave no thought to all the garbage the carnal mind wanted to hit him with at every turn. Paul was a completely changed Person after his conversion.

IMAGINE YOUR OWN LIFE, COMPLETELY GIVEN OVER TO GOD LIVING THROUGH . . . YOU!!

Here's your key, right here, as to how and why you can heal yourself: you already have your healing, it's already done. Jesus made you a brand new person in your spirit.

ONE NEW MAN

For he is our peace, who hath made both one, and hath broken down the middle wall of partition between us; [15] Having abolished in his flesh the enmity, even the law of commandments contained in ordinances; for to make in himself of twain one new man, so making peace; [16] And that he might reconcile both unto God in one body by the cross, having slain the enmity thereby: [17] And came and preached peace to you which were afar off, and to them that were nigh.

Ephesians 2:14-17 KJV

PAUL DIDN'T PRAY FOR GOD TO -D-O- ANYTHING!!

He only prayed that the "eyes of your understanding" be opened!

Ephesians 1:18 KJV

"The eyes of your understanding being enlightened; that ye may know what is the hope of his calling, and what the riches of the glory of his inheritance in the saints."

PAUL PRAYED THAT GOD WOULD LET US SEE THAT WE ALREADY HAVE SUPERNATURAL POWER ON THE INSIDE OF US —

Even before we had a need, we already had everything on the inside of us to last the rest of our lives and way, way beyond!

Colossians 1:27 KJV

To whom God would make known what is the riches of the glory of this mystery among the Gentiles; which is Christ in you, the hope of glory:

CHRIST IS ALREADY IN US !!

"Beloved, the symptoms in your body may be there, but they're not truth. God's Word IS TRUTH. And God says, "By Jesus' stripes, you are healed!" (see 1Pet2:24)

Joseph Prince

YOU CAN HAVE WHAT YOU SAY !

"You can have what you say. The woman who touched Jesus' garment received exactly what she said. The Bible says, "for she said, If I may touch but his clothes, I shall be whole" (v. 28). What she said was her faith speaking. I know it was, for Jesus said, "Daughter, thy faith hath made thee whole" (v. 34). What you say is your faith speaking. You can have what you say. MARK 11:23–24 23 For verily I say unto you, That whosoever shall say unto this mountain, Be thou removed, and be thou cast into the sea; and shall not doubt in his heart, but shall believe that those things which he saith shall come to pass; he shall have whatsoever he saith. 24 Therefore I say unto you, What things soever ye desire, when ye pray, believe that ye receive them, and ye shall have them."

You Can Have What You Say!"

Kenneth E. Hagin [82]

HOW – PLEASE TELL ME HOW – I CAN FINALLY "GET IT"?

ANSWER: BY SUBSTITUTING YOUR NAME EVERYWHERE IN THE BIBLE: "I, Robin Starbuck, AM NOT CEASING TO GIVE THANKS TO YOU, GOD!!" . . . [OR] . . . "MAKING MENTION OF Robin Starbuck . . . ."

Ephesians 1:16 NET

I do not cease to give thanks for you when I remember you in my prayers.

(A word of caution, don't forget that the Bible was, in fact, written to a specific audience, 2,000 years ago, in a language and environment most unlike our own; but that need not interfere with our making application of the spiritual principles laid down.)

* Now I ask you how in the world does he believe he has made himself receptive to healing? He has sabotaged his every attempt! He's ignored every directive, if he's even read them at all. Maybe now he would like to put a little paint thinner into the cake mix, to make it appear smoother!

* To make a cake or pursue a healing, you need to read the instructions carefully and follow them to a tee. Nothing less is indicated. Especially the one about cooking on low heat, for a full hour.

* When you've obeyed all the instructions regarding self-healing then DO NOT DISTURB your healing-in-progress. Don't talk about it or otherwise sabotage your

former declarations of perfection over it. It's critical to understand that you have the power to nullify all the good that you previously accomplished.

* HEALING IS DECEPTIVELY SIMPLE. It is ourselves who make it seem complicated.

* All that is needed is for us to take our feeble grasp of the things of God to the next realm – the place where healing is the norm and all prayers are answered.

AFFIRMATION

"I am not in my body and I am not my body. I am living my Father's life and He is living my life: I and my Father are One. God is the life of me, the being of me, the soul of me: my body is the temple of the living God."

Alright, we're agreed on what it is that we're NOT interested in; now how can we heal our bodies, minds, relationships, jobs, etc.? We already know that we need a working relationship with God. And we already know that, in reality, we don't actually lack anything. We're starting to be okay with the seeming discrepancy! If you'll suspend ALL JUDGEMENT as you continue to read, it will change you. If you don't, you'll most definitely miss out!

Imagine going to Company A in hopes of getting a job. You'd like to be an assistant to the Assistant in charge of Project B, but you're offered a position in the mail room instead.

Then you hear, somewhere in your spirit, that you should accept the opening in the mail room and see if the company has any training programs for its employees. There's one just starting up so you (a) pay the fees to get in and buy the materials needed (b) suspend your usual after-work activities indefinitely, and (c) attend the classes, do the homework, do your work in the mail room - all with a very good, cheerful attitude.

Long story short - six months later you're made Vice President, assisting only the President. Aren't you glad you trusted the Holy Spirit nudging you all the way? This is the kind of listening we're talking about!

CHAPTER 21: Now you try it!

Let's continue with Ephesians: 1:17-18 KJV

That the God of our Lord Jesus Christ, the Father of glory, may give unto you -YOUR NAME- the spirit of wisdom and revelation in the knowledge of him: [18] The eyes of -YOUR NAME's - understanding being enlightened; that ye -YOUR NAME - may know what is the hope of his calling, and what the riches of the glory of his inheritance in the saints.

I see progress, YOUR NAME, but then it gets nullified by 'futuristic' declarations. "I've just got to...." No!! You're already there. You don't have to do anything. Realize right now that you're there right now. Your mind can't trick you. Nothing and nobody can. This is it right here, right now, no future at all – just Spirit, God, good … including and especially … you!

CAN WE TAKE IT TO THE NEXT LEVEL?

Let's use our exceedingly great power which God used to raise Jesus from the dead and which we have on the inside of ourselves.

Ephesians 1:19-20 KJV

And what is the exceeding greatness of his power to us-ward who believe, according to the working of his mighty power, [20] Which he wrought in Christ, when he raised him from the dead, and set him at his own right hand in the heavenly places.

But, how can you ... little ol' you with precious little experience connecting with the Creator of the universe ... appeal to God, Himself, on an ongoing, moment-by-moment basis? Boy, have I got good news for you!

Have you ever heard of the phenomenon called "speaking in tongues" or "praying in tongues"? It's in the Bible, so of course it's hotly debated over! Some say it was only for the generation of people who were around at the time of the Pentecost. Others have made up their own rules and regulations surrounding its usage, but I say let's go for it! Let's use it with abandon to joyfully connect with Papa (Abba) and really have some fun with Him! Even quantum physics, will shed some amazing light (my own personal finding!!) on this glorious gift from God.

QUANTUM PHYSICS, WITH ITS EMPHASIS ON EXPANSION, PAVES THE WAY FOR A BETTER UNDERSTANDING OF THE MIRACULOUS POWER THAT PRAYING IN TONGUES WIELDS BY SPEAKING THE HIDDEN WISDOM OF GOD

1 Corinthians 2:7 KJV

But we speak the wisdom of God in a mystery, even the hidden wisdom, which God ordained before the world unto our glory:

YOU'LL BECOME AMAZINGLY COMFORTABLE WITH THE "MYSTERIES" OF GOD !!

1 Corinthians 14:2 KJV

For he that speaketh in an unknown tongue speaketh
not unto men, but unto God: for no man understandeth
him; howbeit in the spirit he speaketh mysteries.

Speaking/praying "in tongues" is a powerful shortcut to
putting yourself and/or your patient in the realm of
God. When your mind is clouded with negativity, do you
think you'd be cheating if you just jump into tongues?
Of course not! Remember, it's not your mind, but
God's, that jumpstarts this glorious process!!

IT'S YOUR SPIRIT THAT PRAYS !!

1 Corinthians 14:14 KJV

For if I pray in an unknown tongue, my spirit prayeth,
but my understanding is unfruitful.

There's nothing weird or other-worldly about asking
God for an interpretation. He'll put it in simple English,
and immediately.

PRAY, OR SIMPLY ASK, FOR AN INTERPRETATION TO
WHAT GOD HAS IMPLANTED IN YOUR SPIRIT WHILE
YOU WERE SPEAKING IN TONGUES!!

1 Corinthians 14:13 KJV

Wherefore let him that speaketh in an unknown tongue
pray that he may interpret. It will be instantaneously
effective!

Robin's Way of doing Tongues:

Give it a melody. That's right, sing it out! Hey, now don't go running away just because I mentioned "sing" and you think you're no Frank Sinatra! You can sing, or hum, "Happy Birthday", can't you? Try substituting sounds for the words:

HA... PY... BI... DA... TU... YU...

La.... Ve.... Ri... Ga... Mu... Ta....

THERE, YOU JUST DID TONGUES AND IT WAS EASY AND FUN. KEEP IT UP! KEEP IT UP! KEEP GOING. . !! . Keep substituting your own sounds.... WOW!! . You're doing it!

Now, with no effort on your part whatsoever, simply ask God what He just imputed to your spirit. Isn't it WONDERFUL!! . You can do this anytime at all, anyplace, anywhere. You know why? Remember my mentioning humming? You can actually hum so softly that it's entirely inaudible to anyone right next to you. You wanna know if that "counts", lol, ask God: He's put something beautiful in your spirit even as we speak! In summary,

THE MIND OF CHRIST IS ON THE INSIDE OF YOU. HOW DO YOU ACCESS IT? . BY SPEAKING OR PRAYING (or singing) IN TONGUES.

DO YOU HAVE A QUICK TEST that you can apply anytime, anyplace, anywhere, which will reveal to you your present measure of connectedness in the Holy Spirit?

Yes, here's THE ACID TEST:

It is the most useful thing that you could possibly sport because you really need to know this statistic in order to function adequately. What good is having the Holy Spirit if He is not FULLY open to you at any given moment?

Tell me you're not one of those flippers that go back and forth, in and out, a moment here, a moment there. Tell me you're not satisfied selling yourself so short. Yes, He's in you – Hallelujah – what now? A visit from time to time?

There is an instantaneously accessible litmus test that will break through all the ambiguity, uncertainty, doubt and fear: How Do I Know That I Am Fully Aware of my Being in The Spirit?

ANSWER: Make a list of all the people that you are unable to love unconditionally just as much as you love God. When the tally reaches zero, congratulations, you're there!

"It is almost sadness to my soul that men should be astonished and surprised at an ordinary, tangible evidence of the power of God."

~ John G. Lake [83]

SO, YOU'RE TRYING TO HEAL yourself, are you? .

* You've focused all your attention on your ...

First mistake!

Take the full power of God to bear on your issue.
Overwhelm the claim.

* You're telling it that you have suffered with it long
enough ...

Second mistake!

See perfection right there INSTEAD OF anything unlike
God, Spirit.

* You've finished with that treatment and are starting
to think Oh gosh I've got all these annoying ...

Third mistake!

You haven't been on top of things long enough or you
would be aglow with joy and sweetness and light and
love - so much so that nothing, absolutely nothing, else
would matter.

* You think how stupid you must be to slip up yet again.

Fourth (devastating) mistake!

Don't sabotage all your good work. Stay with God - He'll
pull you through.

* You're starting to forget about the problem?

Congratulations! Mistakes have ceased!

...

You're in the realm now where happiness takes over. Suddenly what's more important to you is to bask in God's resplendent Love. His Grace is at once everywhere! You see everybody - everyone who's ever come to your mind - filled to the brim with God, completely healed, whole, healthy and free - and that includes you!

TO SUMMARIZE: If you focus all your attention on the problem you magnify the problem and shouldn't be surprised if the problem worsens. If you pray 2-3 min and then go away filled with doubt, there's too much weight in the wrong scale. Self-condemnation never healed a thing. But getting your mind off the negative appearances clears the way for your consciousness to fill up with the awareness of God's ever-presence.

I hope that throughout this chapter you have been struck by my claim that what is needed to bring full healing, deliverance and multifarious other miracles into your life is to go much deeper, or higher, or further into your awareness of the Holy Spirit within you. One way that throws the doors wide open is to meditate on the limitless expanse of kingdom glory found in quantum physics.

CHAPTER 22: Understanding and describing reality

Would you join me in a FLIGHT OF FANCY for a moment? Imagine a child having a nightmare.

(A) You see his dream in vivid detail.

(B) You can't seem to wake him up.

He's in grave danger and should remain silent. He can't help it, he's whimpering. That's making him more frightened. Since he won't wake up, you want to guide him in order to remove the horrible stress but he just seems to want to go deeper and deeper into the sordid details of the nightmare in spite of his anguish and ever-increasing fear. Now he can hear your voice: what do you tell him to do? You could try to convince the child to shake himself, even splash water on his face in his dream. But, remember, you couldn't SEEM to wake him, so now is your opportunity to break through his hypnotic spell by convincing him to wake up and that it was never real.

That's what it feels like when someone says that there's so much evil in the world. As with Elisha, opening the eyes of his protégé, so we must divine a way to break through the miasma and usher the patient into supernatural healing.

The full story is as follows:

"Now the king of Syria was making war against Israel; and he consulted with his servants, saying, "My camp will be in such and such a place." [9] And the man of God sent to the king of Israel, saying, "Beware that you do not pass this place, for the Syrians are coming down there." [10] Then the king of Israel sent someone to the place of which the man of God had told him. Thus he warned him, and he was watchful there, not just once or twice. [11] Therefore the heart of the king of Syria was greatly troubled by this thing; and he called his servants and said to them, "Will you not show me which of us is for the king of Israel?" [12] And one of his servants said, "None, my lord, O king; but Elisha, the prophet who is in Israel, tells the king of Israel the words that you speak in your bedroom." [13] So he said, "Go and see where he is, that I may send and get him." And it was told him, saying, "Surely he is in Dothan." [14] Therefore he sent horses and chariots and a great army there, and they came by night and surrounded the city. [15] And when the servant of the man of God arose early and went out, there was an army, surrounding the city with horses and chariots. And his servant said to him, "Alas, my master! What shall we do?" [16] So he answered, "Do not fear, for those who are with us are more than those who are with them." [17] And Elisha prayed, and said, "LORD, I pray, open his eyes that he may see." Then the LORD opened the eyes of the young man, and he saw. And behold, the mountain was full of horses and chariots of fire all around Elisha."

2 Kings 6:8-17 NKJV

TO RECAPITULATE:

Healing requires an inroad. With an overabundance of fear, doubt and unbelief hanging over them, Elisha knew that his servant was serving as a block rather than a helper. But, with eyes opened, jubilation ensued! As we have looked back upon Old Covenant Bible stories for courage in expanding our consciousness of the magnanimous role of healing, so can we turn to the quantum realm for a much-needed boost in our ability to -i-m-a-g-i-n-e-.

Do you dance the Wu Li?

One of the greatest physicists of all, Albert Einstein [84], was perhaps a Wu Li Master. In 1938 he wrote: "Physical concepts are free creations of the human mind, and are not, however it may seem, uniquely determined by the external world. In our endeavor to understand reality we are somewhat like a man trying to understand the mechanism of a closed watch. He sees the face and the moving hands, even hears its ticking, but he has no way of opening the case. If he is ingenious he may form some picture of a mechanism which could be responsible for all the things he observes, but he may never be quite sure his picture is the only one which could explain his observations. He will never be able to compare his picture with the real mechanism and he cannot even imagine the possibility of the meaning of such a comparison."

A MODICUM OF HUMILITY is a natural attribute of being filled with awe as it is generally believed that physicists are forever occupied with explaining the world. While less enlightened physicists even believe that, it is the Wu Li Masters who know they are only dancing with it.

QUANTUM DIMENSIONS OF THE SPIRIT

How, then, can a meager knowledge of quantum phenomena enhance one's grasp on the healing aspect of subatomic dimensions? Let's see how Annette Capps characterizes her experience:

"Being the daughter of Charles Capps, how many times do you think I have heard that "things obey words"? Many times, I can assure you! Well, bringing things down to their atomic level and learning that scientifically these particles respond to people, has had a significant effect on my faith. When Jesus spoke to the fig tree and said, "Let no one eat fruit from you ever again" (Mark 11:14), then that fig tree dried up from the atomic level because of His words. When He spoke to the winds and the waves, they obeyed Him. He was teaching us the undeniable Biblical principle that THINGS OBEY WORDS. Jesus did not demonstrate this just to prove He was the Son of God. He demonstrated it and then told his disciples that they too can speak words of power. He wanted us to have the revelation that we are powerful spirit beings who can speak to the mountains in our life and they will obey us."

Annette Capps [85]

Quantum Faith

Things don't just drop into our material realm overnight. We need to hold ourselves more accountable for the way we interact with things in our environment. We may think that it's only a cat or dog, tree or chair, but things do have a way of picking up on our thinking about them. Don't curse anything or anyone with negative thoughts, as if they were our own private domain. Especially now that we've become more enlightened, let's put back into the world good feelings and perceptions about all upon whom our thoughts rest, yes, even our enemies. After all to love our enemies is tantamount to having no enemies!

LOOK SUBATOMICALLY DEEPER.

It hardly takes an astro-physicist or a quantum physicist to speculate that things which we had to accept on faith in the past will gradually become common knowledge.

THE STUFF THAT YOU'RE MADE FROM

And the Maker of the stuff

Are One.

It's you.

Any individual, dedicated to God to such an extent that they have given up the personal sense of life, becomes a healer. There's no other way to become a healer except to have a purified consciousness. Only those who have come to a life devoid of self desire, self will, self glory, self riches, self righteousness, only that state of consciousness becomes the transparency for healing. All other consciousness is just human consciousness of "I, me, and my" - human consciousness, not healing consciousness! You can be a transparency for God knowing that God's presence is already here but must be consciously realized.

When the actual presence of God - not just thinking about God - comes to you, you have entered spiritual life. Until then, you're the "natural man" whom Paul says is not under the law of God, neither indeed can be.

A stirring will take place within you. God's life becomes your life and you no longer have a life of your own. You'll then see that this life that you're living ... is God! Surrender the belief that you were born on a certain date and will die on a certain date and assume your immortality which is yours, not after you die, but before you were born. You can't make it so: it already is so. You don't make it so through being good: you merely discover that it is so. "I live, yet not I; Christ lives as me." "I am come that you might have life and that you might have life more abundantly." That was God speaking through Jesus. "I can of mine own self do nothing."

God, the Father, always announces Himself so that you'll know it's God. There is only one source of your life - God: "Fear not, I am with you." My presence goes before you. My kingdom is established within you. I, Me, My = God. His kingdom is within you and flows from within you.

For effective HEALING

Don't think there's nothing

You can do.

Instead try to find yourself

Wanting to be shown

How to think.

How to feel, how to see,

How to dis-cover

How to love.

Even with a bodily upsetment

There's no way there could be

None in your heart.

Hatred in the mind translates

As surely as a December morn

To hurt-red in your soul.

Wanna know HOW TO love

Absolutely everyone?

Leave the realm of duality.

Opt for the resplendent realm

Where there's only Spirit, God,

Healing and love.

...

Taking a look at HEALING from a multidimensional perspective, our imaginations may be drawn to places where time and space is of no event. We can romp about effortlessly and see our Father's creation from the vantage point of spiritual reality. We don't "know" - as in, squeeze our brains to eke out a modicum of self-assurance; but we KNOW that God is all around and all through us and that we're living our eternal life right now.

Here comes the rub. We have to go back to our little material, disease-laden, ego-driven, accident-prone lives, don't we? My vote is on 'No, we don't!'

Why should we go back and deny everything that we've learned to be true about God? Go back and resume our hurting, hating and suffering? Why not stay in full conscious awareness of our ONENESS with God? Why not remember that we are located behind our eyes and that's why we see perfectly. We hear with the hearing of Christ, which never has to wane. The Holy Spirit breathes through us; we're filled and we send His love out to the world.

We see "the world" quite a bit differently by now, and what a beautiful sight it is! We no longer have issues, for they have vanished. Everyone we can possibly bring to our consciousness - past, present and future - receives an holy kiss, and is joyfully blessed. Amen.

One word has been jumping out at me really big all morning: DESIRE. I'm talking about a good, godly desire such as: "I desire to have my thinking made more godlike." Or, "I desire to love people 100% more than I do." Or, "I desire to 'see' spiritually so clearly that I can bring it to bear on anyone who is hurting." This is the most powerfully effective prayer known to mankind. It simply must have signs following.

The second part of this word-jumping-out- at-me is ... please, please, please don't misunderstand ... : AS WE TAKE OUR FIRST FEW STEPS to do what we can humanly to fulfill such righteous desires, the Holy Spirit totally takes over and puts everything in place 'in the twinkling of an eye'!

ON A MUCH HIGHER PLANE

There is

No ego

Left in me.

It received

Walking papers.

At 4:35 a.m.

The ego

Finally fled

To the native

Nothingness

From whence

It came.

Poesy could

Not contain it,

Human striving too.

That hydra-headed

Ego now at last

Is dead.

...

CHAPTER 23: Hidden Opportunities

Is there still that one damnable issue - and person - that you can't shake? It's so horrible that there's no way you can let go and be fully functional. Why? Why? Why you? Shouldn't you have received your freedom, your healing, by now?

THIS INTERMINABLE VEXATION IS YOUR TICKET TO A WHOLE NEW DIMENSION.

Most people in their entire lifetimes do not penetrate that dimension, so impressed are they with the realm of the mundane. But it's that very real - almost tangible - prolonged angst - that can be utilized to take one deep into the realm of Spirit, God.

God doesn't deliberately burden us with pain and suffering, but we can use such conditions as opportunities to go infinitely deeper in our apprehension of the Absolute, the Spiritual realm of the Real.

A drop of water,

Like the entire ocean,

Is water.

That unforgivable person,

Like all God's creation,

Is God.

Perfect as He in every way,

Despite what all the

Skeptics say.

...

* IN THE -R-E-A-L-M- OF THE SPIRIT *

Therefore, there is now no condemnation for those who are in Christ Jesus,

[2] because through Christ Jesus the law of the Spirit who gives life has set you free from the law of sin and death.

[3] For what the law was powerless to do because it was weakened by the flesh, God did by sending his own Son in the likeness of sinful flesh to be a sin offering. And so he condemned sin in the flesh,

[4] in order that the righteous requirement of the law might be fully met in us, who do not live according to the flesh but according to the Spirit.

[5] Those who live according to the flesh have their minds set on what the flesh desires; but those who live in accordance with the Spirit have their minds set on what the Spirit desires.

[6] The mind governed by the flesh is death, but the mind governed by the Spirit is life and peace.

[7] The mind governed by the flesh is hostile to God; it does not submit to God's law, nor can it do so.

[8] Those who are in the realm of the flesh cannot please God.

[9] You, however, are not in the realm of the flesh but are in the realm of the Spirit, if indeed the Spirit of God lives in you. And if anyone does not have the Spirit of Christ, they do not belong to Christ.

[10] But if Christ is in you, then even though your body is subject to death because of sin, the Spirit gives life because of righteousness. [11] And if the Spirit of him who raised Jesus from the dead is living in you, he who raised Christ from the dead will also give life to your mortal bodies because of his Spirit who lives in you.

[12] Therefore, brothers and sisters, we have an obligation---but it is not to the flesh, to live according to it.

[13] For if you live according to the flesh, you will die; but if by the Spirit you put to death the misdeeds of the body, you will live.

[14] For those who are led by the Spirit of God are the children of God.

[15] The Spirit you received does not make you slaves, so that you live in fear again; rather, the Spirit you received brought about your adoption to sonship. And by him we cry, "Abba, Father."

[16] The Spirit himself testifies with our spirit that we are God's children. [17] Now if we are children, then we are heirs---heirs of God and co-heirs with Christ, if indeed we share in his sufferings in order that we may also share in his glory.

[18] I consider that our present sufferings are not worth comparing with the glory that will be revealed in us.

[19] For the creation waits in eager expectation for the children of God to be revealed.

[20] For the creation was subjected to frustration, not by its own choice, but by the will of the one who subjected it, in hope

[21] that the creation itself will be liberated from its bondage to decay and brought into the freedom and glory of the children of God.

[22] We know that the whole creation has been groaning as in the pains of childbirth right up to the present time.

[23] Not only so, but we ourselves, who have the firstfruits of the Spirit, groan inwardly as we wait eagerly for our adoption to sonship, the redemption of our bodies.

[24] For in this hope we were saved. But hope that is seen is no hope at all. Who hopes for what they already have?

[25] But if we hope for what we do not yet have, we wait for it patiently.

[26] In the same way, the Spirit helps us in our weakness. We do not know what we ought to pray for, but the Spirit himself intercedes for us through wordless groans.

[27] And he who searches our hearts knows the mind of the Spirit, because the Spirit intercedes for God's people in accordance with the will of God.

[28] And we know that in all things God works for the good of those who love him, who have been called according to his purpose.

[29] For those God foreknew he also predestined to be conformed to the image of his Son, that he might be the firstborn among many brothers and sisters.

[30] And those he predestined, he also called; those he called, he also justified; those he justified, he also glorified.

[31] What, then, shall we say in response to these things? If God is for us, who can be against us?

[32] He who did not spare his own Son, but gave him up for us all---how will he not also, along with him, graciously give us all things?

[33] Who will bring any charge against those whom God has chosen? It is God who justifies.

[34] Who then is the one who condemns? No one. Christ Jesus who died---more than that, who was raised to life---is at the right hand of God and is also interceding for us.

 [35] Who shall separate us from the love of Christ? Shall trouble or hardship or persecution or famine or nakedness or danger or sword?

[36] As it is written: "For your sake we face death all day long; we are considered as sheep to be slaughtered."

[37] No, in all these things we are more than conquerors through him who loved us.

[38] For I am convinced that neither death nor life, neither angels nor demons, neither the present nor the future, nor any powers,

[39] neither height nor depth, nor anything else in all creation, will be able to separate us from the love of God that is in Christ Jesus our Lord.

Romans 8:1-39 NIV

...

(A) i can prove God doesn't heal.

(B) how?

(A) he has never healed me.

(B) have you prayed without ceasing?

(A) well, no.

(B) have you, in all humility, asked him?

(A) not exactly.

(B) what exactly HAVE you done?

(A) nothing. just waiting for God.

(B) God's part is done.

(B) God created you perfect.

(B) God is on the inside of you.

(B) right now you're breathing God.

(B) when you see, you're seeing God.

(B) when you hear, you're hearing God.

(B) when you love, you'll see you're healed.

...

ANOTHER THOUGHT ON THE SUBJECT OF HEALING

When we ever so wisely turn to God

Instead of the apothecaries

And we pray with all due diligence

For a longstanding and/or urgent need

We praise Him for 'already' having healed the malady

2,000 plus years ago,

We fill our hearts, minds and souls

With the metaphysical Truth serum of our benevolent, ever loving Father.

We look to the high heaven and praise the Lord for His infinite, unwavering goodness.

And when we've accomplished all that

We examine our body and "observe"

That the lies of the carnal mind and their manifestations

Are still there. So, we vow to do better next time

To think harder

To pray better

To sing louder

What, actually,

Was our mistake?

It occurred when "We examined our body and "observed" ...

Translation:

We allowed a flood of negativity in and gave it full reign,

Bowed down to it

And in a nanosecond

Denied every one of the real truths

That we had iterated above

And that we should have stuck with.

...

DO IT AFRAID!!!

When a fearful, unkind or unpleasant thought drops into your head and you summarily dismiss it, it doesn't move on to the next unsuspecting victim; it doesn't go anywhere because you have destroyed it! Does Fear rule in your life? When you know that you're right with God, and you know that what you want to do is also right with God *BUT* you feel afraid... Go ahead and do it! DO IT AFRAID!! Doing so will lead you right out of fear. You have just begun to share in what Gregg Braden dubs the Divine Matrix, i.e., to "share life-affirming practices that come from a unified quantum worldview":

"Just as all life is built from the four chemical bases that create our DNA, the universe appears to be founded upon four characteristics of the Divine Matrix that make things work in the way they do. The key to tapping the power of the Matrix lies in our ability to embrace the four landmark discoveries that link it to our lives in an unprecedented way:

Discovery 1: There is a field of energy that connects all of creation.

Discovery 2: This field plays the role of a container, a bridge, and a mirror for the beliefs within us.

Discovery 3: The field is nonlocal and holographic. Every part of it is connected to every other, and each piece mirrors the whole on a smaller scale.

Discovery 4: We communicate with the field through the language of emotion. It's our power to recognize and apply these realities that determine everything from our healing to the success of our relationships and careers. Ultimately, our survival as a species may be directly linked to our ability and willingness to share life-affirming practices that come from a unified quantum worldview."

Gregg Braden [86]

THE DIVINE MATRIX:

Bridging time, space,

miracles and belief

Psalm 27:1 KJV

The Lord is my light and my salvation; whom shall I fear? the Lord is the strength of my life; of whom shall I be afraid?

Psalm 27:1 AMP

THE LORD is my Light and my Salvation—whom shall I fear or dread? The Lord is the Refuge and Stronghold of my life—of whom shall I be afraid?

CHAPTER 24: Conclusions

It works!! It really, really works!! If you want healing, affirm God. God is in you and you are in God. Just keep affirming and affirming and affirming. God is in me and I am in God. God is in my stomach, in my lungs in my nostrils. He is in that person whom I have trouble with, and all that I can see when I think of them is God. No ungodly thought had better even try to enter this perfect mind. I am God's. All around me everything I see, everything I think about is God. This is the new heaven and new earth. This is God's kingdom here and now with everything and everyone in it perfect. We get to see this as we open our eyes, our spiritual eyes. God is in our stuff, our perfectly healed computers and phones, TVs, everything. Whatever I can see is God. Whatever I can think about is God. Anyone who can see me with their eyes or in their minds can see only God because God is all that there is. There is not a single issue out there that cannot be completely healed, thoroughly loved, wonderfully adored because it is all God. God is my Papa and my brother and my sister and my child. There is absolutely nothing that God cannot heal instantaneously. Absolutely nothing!! God IS Love.

...

What I wrote above - in deepest gratitude - is what I think of as an APPLICATION of John 15:5 and many, many other glorious scriptures. I made it my own. Miracles started to pour in. Then I acted as scribe and tried to recapture my application for anyone who might benefit.

John 15:5 NIV

"I am the vine; you are the branches. If you remain in me and I in you, you will bear much fruit; apart from me you can do nothing."

A FOLLOW-UP TO "IT WORKS!!"

When you've read through "It Works" and made it your own by affirming the overwhelming Allness of God everywhere in your life . . .

And . . .

You've enjoyed some wonderful breakthroughs beyond your wildest dreams . . .

When all of that is over . . .

And the thrill is starting to subside . . .

BE WARNED!!! . . .

SUBSIDING IS UNACCEPTABLE!!!

Subsiding is no part of God.

God is all about expanding, accelerating, and experiencing more, more, more!

What should you do? Even this:

GO BACK TO THE DRAWING BOARD!! . . .

Commit yourself to starting all over exactly the same way, leaving out nothing; and, as you do exactly that, the Holy Spirit will take over. It will not take anywhere near as long. You will get right back to where you were when you were first highly exhilarated. Celebrate yet another major victory, for you have arrived yet again. And then it lasts longer but eventually stuff gets in the way. Go back! Go back! Go back! It's way, way, way too important to give it a back seat! Do it again and it will be even easier and more natural. And another celebration! Keep doing this until you no longer have to face the prospect of the inspiration subsiding.

...

TO CJH: I hear you loud and clear and can easily sympathize with you. But, to tell you the truth, sympathy is the last thing that could help you. Did you see my follow-up to this post? You have inspired me right here to write a second follow-up or a part 3!! What I would say in part 3 is that if you look to the body as much as 51% you are putting more weight into the scale of the problem and it would be no surprise for the problem to persist. I would recommend checking out part 2 and do it with the ideas that I'm mentioning here in mind. You need consistency and persistence and you cannot take it lightly or the least bit jokingly. If you focus on the problem you will enhance the problem. You need to do more affirmations like the ones I wrote above only make them your own personal affirmations, knowing God as well as you do. You know the nature of God. You can completely absolutely heal the entire body and everything else in your life that needs healing. It doesn't have to take time but it does require a complete commitment. Lots of love to you.

BUT, NOW, I SEE!!

Amazing Grace, how sweet the sound,

That saved a wretch like me -

I once was lost but now am found,

Was blind, but now, I see.

T'was Grace that taught -

my heart to fear.

And Grace, my fears relieved.

How precious did that Grace appear -

the hour I first believed.

Through many dangers, toils and snares -

we have already come.

T'was Grace that brought us safe thus far -

and Grace will lead us home.

The Lord has promised good to me -

His word my hope secures.

He will my shield and portion be -

as long as life endures.

When we've been here ten thousand years -

bright shining as the sun.

We've no less days to sing God's praise -

then when we've first begun.

Amazing Grace, how sweet the sound,

That saved a wretch like me -

I once was lost but now am found,

Was blind, BUT NOW, I SEE. [87]

...

LOSE YOUR INTEREST IN "HOW" EVERYTHING WILL
WORK OUT!! Psalm 103:12 KJV

As far as the east is from the west, so far hath he
removed our transgressions from us.

. IN THE BEGINNING, G-O-D!!

. IN THE MIDDLE, GOD!!

. IN THE -O-N-L-Y-, GOD!!

. JUST LET IT GO!!

. FORGIVE EVERYONE !!

. REJOICE!!

...

SO VERY FOCUSED

I beg you, please don't take this the wrong way - you know where I'm coming from. When we LITERALLY would -rather- have the challenge that keeps us nearly 100% on track than the freedom to celebrate re-entrance into distractions, and we just love, love, love our life with God soooo much, well, my whole point is "Aren't we already there?" It's not a competition, but don't we have something that distracted people ... don't? It's just a thought.

...

ARE YOU SOMEWHAT HEALED?

Have you reached the point where you can tolerate the pain, trembling, loss, fear, doubt? Have you told God that you can take it from here?

WHY DON'T YOU ASK GOD WHAT -H-E- WANTS?

3 John 1:2 KJV

Beloved, I wish above all things that thou mayest prosper and be in health, even as thy soul prospereth.

One of the greatest handicaps to full awakening is to think that there is such a thing as a partial awakening or that one would be rewarded for having done a very good job even though he hasn't penetrated the spiritual ultimate of all things.

YOU CAN'T LIE TO GOD: the thought of it is just too ridiculous for words! Can you imagine God not knowing, when God knows everything, every moment, all the time? So don't try to pad your bill to Him and say you did such a good job on this and that and the other.

* There should be no bill (account).

* There should be no pad

* There should just simply be receiving his love, receiving his healing, receiving his words of wisdom - all of which you do by listening.

IF I HAD BEEN ONE OF THE TWELVE (DISCIPLES) WHEN HEARING OF THEIR LORD'S IMPENDING DEATH AND FACED WITH UNSPEAKABLE SORROW, I COULDN'T HAVE DONE ANY BETTER . . . U-N-L-E-S-S- I HAD HAD THE HOLY SPIRIT AS WE DO NOW. IN A FLIGHT OF FANCY, I CAN IMAGINE TRYING TO TURN THE DISCIPLES' EYES TO THE "REAL" JESUS, SPIRITUAL AND PERFECT, AND AWAY FROM A SOON-TO-BE-BROKEN BODY. BUT NOW, PRAISE THE LORD, WE HAVE THIS HOLY SPIRIT LIVING ON THE INSIDE OF OUR BORN AGAIN SPIRITS.

HEALING EXPANDED

TO HEAL YOURSELF - AND BY EXTENSION, THE WORLD - YOU NEED TO BE FILLED TO THE BRIM WITH GOD AND EMPTIED OUT COMPLETELY OF ERROR. THIS BOOK HAS GONE IN EVERY DIRECTION CONCEIVABLE TO REACH THE READER - YOU - WITH THE ASTRONOMICALLY GOOD NEWS: THE ANSWER IS RIGHT HERE!

You don't have to wait a moment

To be with Me.

You don't have to do anything

Whatsoever

To hear my voice.

You are in Me.

And I in you.

I am at once everywhere.

You don't need to get up.

Nor to sit down.

You don't have to close a book.

Nor open one.

Your ability to hear My voice

In your spirit

Is growing by leaps and bounds.

After all,

I am speaking to you right now,

 aren't I?

 …

CHAPTER 25: Quotable Quotes

... of some of Robin's FRIENDS (Sorry I couldn't get everybody in here, but please enjoy this sample):

Enlightenment is when a wave realizes it is the ocean.

--Ian Bentley

The more I read through the Bible the less I have in common with modern Christianity.

--Robert J. Simon

Do you know why I am so fully persuaded of the Sonship/Grace message ....it's because it was revealed to me by the Divine Revelation of The Holy Spirit.

--Joy Williams

"That's why it's very important to study the word on your own, "depending entirely on the holy spirit for interpretation."

--Penelope Masele Kapijimpanga,

Everything you add to the truth, subtracts from the truth

--Elizabeth Cain

Many Christians' definition of "heretic": Someone who knows the Bible better than them.

--Simon Yap

Sometimes I have to stop and think of the tens of thousands of times that I have been forgiven, and I am so thankful.

--Matthew Robert Payne

"LOVE THE LORD THY GOD- it should be noted that the command does not say to love God in good times only.

--Tylene White

When we hear the Word of God speak to us then we finally understand what the Book called the Bible is trying to say!

--Tim Heart

It amazes me how people speak so highly of sickness...

Sickness get under my feet!!

--Jason Fugate

You cannot put God in a theological box - you must encounter him. He is too big to figure out and too vast to put into words. My best efforts to describe him fall short of human words.

--Lynn Hiles

Could it be that God is more loving and accepting than what your theology will allow?

--Henry Harris

Who told you that you weren't good enough?

You did...

--Bruce Harbert

True faith doesn't just wait for the manifestation of what it believes God for... True faith goes looking for the manifestation.

--Cayce Talbott

blogtalkradio

That awesome moment when an elder person says to you, "you got respect, continue like that you got my blessings"

--Kenneth Gaveni Shivambu

Just read an article on the most common use of pliers. It was gripping.

--Mike Carter

We can't say we surrender all and still be holding onto the law.

--Valerie Baard

The law is not equal to Grace

It is the absence of Grace.

--Derrick Day Ministries

Jesus loves you and I do too.

--Jeremiah Johnson

That'll preach someone happy, or mad. Amen or oh me.

--Mark Hicks

I'm a very common man who serves a very uncommon God.

--Allen D. Gee

Simplicity is a major ingredient of the gospel.

--Enejo Adamu

COURAGE IS THE ABILITY TO STILL MOVE FORWARD... IN SPITE OF FEAR.... BE BRAVE!!!!!!

--Stacy Cameron

Until you know and recognize God in ordinary things, you will never know Him in the extraordinary. :-) #DrCC

--Dr. Cindye Coates

"...the salvation of Israel foretold by Paul in Romans 11 would be in fulfillment of Isaiah 27:10, which cites the Song of Moses (Deuteronomy 32)". -

--Dr. Don K. Preston

A nonconformist, irreligious follower of Christ.

--Tomsan Kattackal

So when you see a gift horse... Where exactly should you be looking?

--Russ Lewis

Now is the time to go forward with resolute focus, with truth, trust and passion.

--Tammora Kalis

Don't trust the flesh, trust Grace...he works.

--Eric Rukin

Re String Theory: All those strings that make up the visible Universe, do the stray ones attract each other and make cobwebs?

--Dan Hassett

As my heart is getting more and more established in God's unconditional love and grace for us, I am getting more and more free....

--Tammy Starforth

We serve a God who performs miracles, a powerful God indeed who just heals you by just calling unto his name. Jesus Christ. ..

--Kagiso Mashego

All that I AM and have are of God.

--Muzi Joint Heir Spirit

The salvation event was placed in the past so that Man could not screw it up.

--Bradly Taylor

The manifestation of sonship lies in His presence in us which is as good as his physical presence in the streets of Galilee.

--Simeon Edigbe

A couple of reasons that healing/health can be blocked from being manifested at times is (and I believe this is the biggest one), because of a sense of condemnation as a result of 'feelings' of not being forgiven.

--Dr. Kay Fairchild

The ministration of the Gospel will make you rejoice that you are born gain.

--Steve Chukwudi Fidel

Love you to the bone! rjs: Love you more!

--Gail Ellis

We are full of Him; we shall not hunger, shall not thirst, shall not walk in darkness, shall not lack!

--Mwanga Leonard Arapsotyo

Be there. Or spend the rest of your life wishing that you had been. . . . Michael C King

I have the audacity to believe when Jesus said "IT IS FINISHED" that's exactly what He meant......

--Sheila Welch-Pelot

In my opinion, it is institutional religion that has dominated the pages of church history...

--Timothy King

Here's the secret to living a most fulfilled, peaceful and adventurous life! Learn to face God's faith and not your fears :)

--Francois Du Toit

I bet there are a lot of American Indians who wish they could have screened people coming to their Homeland back during the European invasion.Just saying.

--David Dolejs

To fear God is the beginning of wisdom.

--Angie Morales

Is this a great time to be alive or what?!

--Ernest L. Yates

Fear came knocking at the door

Faith answered

No one there!

--Kent Lindsay

Unless God ceases to be God and breaks His own oath with Himself my salvation is eternally secure and I can be eternally confident in that!! because it is impossible for God to lie.....

--Ranjana Dickenson Sonu

No matter which side of the fence you fall off on this issue .. this is high-larious⊡⊡ I think

--Carol Anderson

I think there are many who would love to speak in tongues but are fearful or embarrassed about asking particular questions!

--Peter Wilson

The destruction of Jerusalem and the Temple are definitely largely and sadly 'overlooked' by the modern day Church today and this is due to a lack of understanding God's Judgment upon his covenant people" according to the flesh' during the Parousia.

--Julienne Chambers

I'm inviting people over to drink coffee and stare at our phones later. ;)

--Brian Bauer

Those that call you deceived are the very ones that have it wrong, but they think they are the only ones that have it right. Lol

--Patricia Harris

If you have kids, they need your affirmation more than they need the things you buy them.

--Tommy Hawk

I have given up all healthy food for Lent.

--Ted Nelson

Not even a law mentality can separate one from Father's love for them....His Mercy and Grace extends far greater than one's limited mind.

--Flora Samuel

Truth is available only to those who have the courage to question whatever they have been taught. Jean N Josh Willis

 I was empty, hurting, religious. Then Creator, God's Son, by His Spirit gave me His Perfect Love.

--Janet Dawson

God will put you where he wants you ... even if no one thinks you deserve the position.

--Irene Geel

--Hurting someone with the truth Is better than making them happy with a lie.

--Sarah Bradt Levesque.

When is this "old enough to know better" supposed to kick in?

--Kathy Hall Harris

The greatest truth sometimes offends.

--John Senior

What you think of your brother is exactly what you are.

--Christel Gast

Ah, the immutable life and rest of finished work. It drives the religious people crazy!

--Monty Dickerson

There are now about 7 billion people on planet Earth, and about 1/3 or 2.2 billion are Christians.

--David Duncan

God's Covenant Journey

Your faith or his faith. Is it finished, or do you have to do something to finish it.

--David Williams

Have you noticed Jesus preferred healing a man/woman than keeping the book? ;)

--Philip George

I'm a heretic yes I know haaa haaa, if you happy and you know it ... !

--Daniel Anderson

"God goes throughout the whole earth, searching to and fro for a heart that will believe him above their experience."

--Erna Atkins

Be of good courage,

And He shall strengthen your heart,

All you who hope in the LORD.

--Heather Creed

Don't ever feel guilty about not being afraid.

--John Ogbu

Yes talk about your joys and all the good in your life!!

--Diane Maartens

Today you will stop living in your past and release the chains that have held you there all this time.

--Ken Etter

Man can not make it without God!

--Sonny Hanna

"Death is a comma not a period."

"Life wins."

--Kathy Jane Nolan

Writers write. Proceed with calm fire. God bless you, Robin Starbuck. :)

--David Martin Stevens

Do not despise reflexion.

--Jean-Pierre Cote

APPENDIX - A – Not "Works", nor human striving, but awareness is indicated. Sincere seekers of Truth everywhere have been coming to the conclusion that human effort, or "works" are contraindicated when it comes to living in the spirit and spending time - a lot of time - with our Papa, Abba, God. He wants us happy and sharing our joy with Him so of course He's not about driving us through guilt and punishment to do his bidding ... hardly!!! But sometimes people read things that I've written and misconstrue them because I tell them there's a great deal that they can do to learn about this wonderful God that we have. They tend to take it as meaning that they should work hard in order to win God's approval or to gain salvation or to appease his anger. This is so far from what I want to convey that I finally sent out the following stream-of-consciousness plea for help in getting it across to the reader that works is not the way to God's heart. God lives in us and the only striving that we need to do is to learn about this glorious fact.

I NEED YOUR HELP!!!

 I'm writing this as stream-of consciousness kind of rambling. as most of you know I'm trying to finish writing a book that I've been working on for quite a long time. I am desperate to get it right. I'm talking about the overall message to the reader that's what I want to be sure to get right. most people steer clear of attempting to teach people how to heal themselves, so guess what the robin chooses to write about!! I need to get it really really clear that of course I know that it's God that does the healing and to be sure I did say so in the book. but what has come to my attention now is that people are going to read into it that I am about a Works type of approach and that's exactly what I am NOT about. what I want the reader to know is that healing is very very possible and normal and indicated as such in the Bible. So when people preach don't do anything do absolutely nothing there is nothing that you need to do, the sufferer is left with nothing. there is so much that the person in need can do and it's not about a Works oriented approach. God does the work. God does the healing. Does the person who is asking you for help understand this or does the person think that if they try to do anything at all they are somehow trapped in a whole new kind of legalism where the right thing to do is to do absolutely nothing? there is a crying need for awareness, the person can do a lot to bring him or herself into awareness. they can ask God to reveal to them exactly what would be most suitable for them to do and if it is to sit and do absolutely nothing then and only then would that be absolutely fine. they need to know about God's love and God's willingness to heal. as they strive to know God better that action pushes out contrary beliefs and activities and that is pretty wonderful. it's not about works it's about getting oneself to a point of being able to hear God's voice and recognizing that God resides right on the inside of them.

They don't have to go anywhere or do anything except that they do need to be made aware so when people criticize those of us who are saying yes there is something you can do and that doing is to open your heart and open your mind to God's omnipotence and omnipresent and omniscience. reading and studying and listening and asking God to reveal himself is not a damnable Works oriented approach the fact is that God lives on the inside of every single one of us and we just have to become aware of it. For some people that entails sitting completely still and meditating; but for other people it means opening a book a Bible a commentary other books on the subject there's nothing wrong with making a supreme effort to get to know this wonderful wonderful wonderful God who lives on the inside of you - and slapping a label on a person who is trying to do so is so cruel it's like a whole new legalism. People can learn how to heal yes of course that is to say How to connect in such a way as to avail themselves of this precious gift from God. what could be better for a person to do then to strive to get to know this God that inheres on the inside of him or her and is more than happy to heal.

BIBLIOGRAPHY

Beebe, L. (1983) Risk-taking and the language learner. In
H. Seliger and M. Long (Eds.), Classroom Oriented
Research in Second Language Acquisition. Rowley,
Mass.: Newberry House.

Bohr, Niels (1958) Atomic Physics and Human
Knowledge New York (Edited by John Wiley and Sons).

Braden, Gregg (2009) The Spontaneous Healing of Belief
Carlsbad, California Hay House.

Celce-Murcia, M. & Larsen-Freeman, D. (1983). The
Grammar Book: An ESL/EFL Teacher's Course. Rowley,
Mass., Newberry House.

Corder, S. (1971). Idiosyncratic dialects and error
analysis. International Review of Applied Linguistics in
Language Teaching [IRAL], 9(2).

Crisco, Chuck, Master of Divinity, Doctorate in Ministry,
aNewDayDawning.

Dickerson, L. (1975) Interlanguage as a system of
variable rules. TESOL Quarterly, 9.

Einstein, A., and Infeld, L., The Evolution of Physics, New
York, Simon & Schuster, 1961.

Eisenstein, M. & Berkowitz,D. (1981). The effect of
phonological variation on adult learner comprehension.
Studies in Second Language Acquisition, 4 (1).

Eisenstein, Miriam R. (1982). A study of social variation in adult second language acquisition. Language Learning, 32,(2).

Eisenstein, M. R. (1983). Native reactions to non-native speech: A review of empirical research. Studies in Second Language Acquisition, 5(2).

Eisenstein, M. & Hopper, S. (1983). The intelligibility of English dialects for adult Learners of English as a second language. Indian Journal of Applied Linguistics, 9.

Eisenstein, Miriam & Verdi, G. (1985). The intelligibility of social dialects for working-class adult Learners of English. Language Learning, 35(2).

Goethe, Theory of Colours, (trans, Eastlake, C.L., London, 1840: repr. M.I.T. Press, Cambridge, Mass., 1970).

Goldsmith, Joel S., American spiritual author, teacher, spiritual healer, modern day mystic. Founded The Infinite Way Movement. Practicing the Presence.

Goswami, Amit (1993) The Self-Aware Universe: How Consciousness Creates the Material World Los Angeles, J.P Tarcher.

Goswami, Amit (2008) God is not Dead: What Quantum Physics Tells Us About Our Origins and How We Should Live Charlottesville, Virginia, Hampton Roads Publishing Company.

Greene, Brian (1999) The Elegant Universe New York, W.W. Norton & Co.

Greene, Brian (2005 The Fabric of the Cosmos Vintage Books.

Hawking, Stephen (2007) God Created the Integers New York, Running Press.

Heisenberg, Werner (1971) Physics and Beyond New York, HarperCollins Publishers.

] Josephus, Flavius (AD37-100), (Historical accounts of the Jewish War. Historian and General in Army)

Keathley, Dr. Don, President, Global Grace Seminary; Founder/Senior Pastor at Grace Point Community Church; Studied at Olivet Nazarene University; Studied at Barnham Graduate School and Seminary; Studied Systematic Theology at Olivet Nazarene University.

Krashen, S., Houck, N., Giunchi, P., Bode, S., Birnbaum, R., & Strei, J. (1977). Difficulty order for grammatical morphemes for adult second language performers using free speech. TESOL Quarterly, 11, 338-41.

_____. (1978). The Monitor Model for second-language acquisition. In R. Gingras (Ed.), Second language acquisition and foreign language teaching (pp.1-26). Arlington, Virginia: Center for Applied Linguistics.

_____. (1981a). Second language acquisition and second language learning. Oxford: Pergamon Press.

_____. (1982). Principles and practice in second language acquisition. Oxford: Pergamon Press.

Labov, W. (1966). Social Stratification of English in New York City. Washington, D.C.: Center for Applied Linguistics.

_____. (1970). The study of language in its social context. Studium Generale 23.

_____. (1972). Sociolinguistic patterns. Philadelphia: University of Pennsylvania Press.

_____. (Ed.). (1980). Locating language in time and space. New York: Academic Press.

Lantolf, J.P. & Khanji, R. (1983). Non-linguistic parameters of interlanguage performance: Expanding the research paradigm. In J. Morreall (Ed.), The Ninth LACUS Forum, 1982. Columbia, s.c.: Hornbeam Press.

Lewis, C.S (1977) The Magician's Nephew New York, Collier Books.

Ochs, E. & Schieffelin, B. (1979). Developmental Pragmatics. New York: Academic Press.

O'Hare, Lee. Artist, spiritual pilgrim.

Quirk, R., Greenbaum, S., Leech, G., & Svartvik, J. (1985). A comprehensive grammar of the english language. New York: Longman.

Richards, J., Platt, J., & Weber, H. (Eds.). (1985). Longman dictionary of applied linguistics. Essex, England: Longman.

Ross, Hugh: (2001) The Creator and the Cosmos (3rd Edition) NavPress, Beyond the Cosmos.

Russell, Bertrand (1918) "The Study of Mathematics," in Mysticism and Logic, and Other Essays, London: Longmans, Green.

Rutherford, Robert, YouTube pastor. Pastor at The Bridge. P.O. Box 3622 Eatonton, GA 31024.

Sato, C. (1985). Task variation in interlanguage phonology. In S. Gass & C. Madden (Eds.), Input in second language acquisition: Series on issues in second language research (pp 181-196). Rowley, Mass.: Newbury House.

Schmidt, R. (1977). Sociolinguistic variation and language transfer in phonology. Working Papers on Bilingualism, 12.

Schrödinger, Erwin: (1983) My View of the World. Woodbridge CT, Ox Bow Press.

Selinker, L. (1972). Interlanguage. International Review of Applied Linguistics in Language Teaching [IRAL], 10.

Tarone, E., (1979). Interlanguage as chameleon. Language Learning, 29(1).

_____. (1982). Systematicity and attention in interlanguage. Language Learning. 32(1), .

_____. (1985). Variability in interlanguage use: A study of style-shifting in morphology and syntax. Language Learning,

Wolfram, W. (1985). Variability in tense marking: A case for the obvious. Language Learning, 35(2)

Wright, Jacob M., The Wright Brothers, thewrightbrothersmusic

Yap, Simon, Lawyer, Blogger, Dark comedian, Hischarisisenough.

Zukav, Gary (1979) The Dancing Wu Li Masters: An Overview of the New Physics New York, HarperCollins.

ENDNOTES

PART ONE: TRADITIONAL RELIGION RENOUNCED

CHAPTER 1: I hate traditional religion too!

[1] Robert Rutherford

YouTube pastor. Pastor at The Bridge. P.O. Box 3622 Eatonton, GA 31024.

[2] Dr. Gary Zukav

The Dancing Wu Li Masters: An Overview of the New Physics.

[3] Josephus, Flavius (AD37-100),

(Historical accounts of the Jewish War. Historian and General in Army)

The End of the Age.

CHAPTER 2: A better approach to interpreting the Bible

[4] Jacob M. Wright, The Wright Brothers, thewrightbrothersmusic.

[5] Dr. Don Keathley, President, Global Grace Seminary; Founder/Senior Pastor at Grace Point Community Church; Studied at Olivet Nazarene University; Studied at Barnham Graduate School and Seminary; Studied Systematic Theology at Olivet Nazarene University.

[6] Joel S. Goldsmith, American spiritual author, teacher, spiritual healer, modern day mystic. Founded The Infinite Way Movement. Practicing the Presence.

CHAPTER 3: Not in your strength.

[7] Chuck Crisco, BA in Bible, Master of Divinity, Doctorate in Ministry, aNewDayDawning.

[8] Herty Afia Tilly, Apostle Tony, Soul Touch International.

[9] Lee O'Hare

CHAPTER 4: Application - This is Your part

[10] Dr. Hugh Ross, Ph.D.

[11] Tim Heart

CHAPTER 5: *Hot Topics* in modern Christianity

[12] Andrew Wommack

[13] Edgar Allen Poe

[14] Paul Ellis

[15] Simon Yap

[16] Jeff Turner

[17] Chuck Crisco

PART TWO: COMMUNICATION GLITCHES

CHAPTER 6: Even the pros have trouble communicating.

[18] Albert Einstein

[19] Werner Heisenberg

[20] Erwin Schrödinger

[21] Isidor I. Rabi

[22] Gary Zukav

CHAPTER 7: Research & analysis

[23] Eisenstein, M. & Berkowitz,D. (1981). The effect of phonological variation on adult learner comprehension. Studies in Second Language Acquisition, 4 (1), 75-80.

_____. (1982). A study of social variation in adult second language acquisition. Language Learning, 32,(2), 367-391.

[24] Tarone, E., (1979). Interlanguage as chameleon. Language Learning, 29(1), 181-191.

Tarone, E., (1982). Systematicity and attention in interlanguage. Language Learning. 32(1), 69-84.

[25] Sato, C. (1985). Task variation in interlanguage phonology. In S. Gass & C. Madden (Eds.), Input in second language acquisition: Series on issues in second language research (pp 181-196). Rowley, Mass.: Newbury House.

[26] Krashen, S., Houck, N., Giunchi, P., Bode, S., Birnbaum, R., & Strei, J. (1977). Difficulty order for

grammatical morphemes for adult second language performers using free speech. TESOL Quarterly, 11, 338-41.

Krashen, Stephen. (1978). The Monitor Model for second-language acquisition. In R. Gingras (Ed.), Second language acquisition and foreign language teaching (pp.1-26). Arlington, Virginia: Center for Applied Linguistics.

Krashen, S. (1981a). Second language acquisition and second language learning. Oxford: Pergamon Press.

Krashen, Stephen. (1982). Principles and practice in second language acquisition. Oxford: Pergamon Press.

[27] James Lantolf 1983.Lantolf, J.P. & Khanji, R. (1983). Non-linguistic parameters of interlanguage performance: Expanding the research paradigm. In J. Morreall (Ed.), The Ninth LACUS Forum, 1982. Columbia, s.c.: Hornbeam Press. (pp. 457-472).

[28] Tarone, E. (1985). Variability in interlanguage use: A study of style-shifting in morphology and syntax. Language Learning, 35(3), 373-403.

[29] Dr. Miriam R. Eisenstein, (1983). Native reactions to non-native speech: A review of empirical research. Studies in Second Language Acquisition, 5(2), 160-176.

_____ & Hopper, S. (1983). The intelligibility of English dialects for adult Learners of English as a second language. Indian Journal of Applied Linguistics, 9, 43-52.

_____ & Verdi, G. (1985). The intelligibility of social dialects for working-class adult Learners of English. Language Learning, 35(2), 287-298.

[30] Dr. Robin Starbuck & Dr. Miriam R. Eisenstein.

CHAPTER 8: Further research & discovery. Participants in survey:

[31] Mike Childers

[32] Timothy Pickering

[33] Brenda Mantooth

[34] Debra Post

[35] Rita Swartz

[36] David Dolejs

[37] John Kemp

[38] Stacy Cameron

[39] Barbara Sternal

[40] Chris Welch

[41] Dan Beloved Resurreccion

[42] Dictionary by Farlex

[43] Andrew Wommack

[44] Mark Hicks

CHAPTER 9: The Study continues ... and concludes.

[45] SPSS Statistics (originally, Statistical Package for the Social Sciences, later modified to read Statistical Product and Service Solutions) was released in its first version in 1968 after being developed by Norman H. Nie, Dale H. Bent, and C. Hadlai Hull. SPSS is among the most widely used programs for statistical analysis in social science.

PART THREE: QUANTUM MECHANICS TO THE RESCUE

CHAPTER 10: Seeing from a new perspective - a real God-perspective!

[46] Einstein

[47] ibid.

[48] Dr. Hugh Ross

[49] Brian Greene

[50] Rudolph Tanzi

[51] Deepak Chopra

[52] Rudolph Tanzi

CHAPTER 11: The Music of the Spheres

[53] Frank Hanks

[54] Phil Mason

[55] Annette Capps

[56] Phil Mason

[57] Max Planck

[58] ibid.

[59] Phil Mason

[60] David Rogstad

[61] ibid.

PART FOUR: QUANTUM PHYSICS EXPANDING

CHAPTER 12: Expanding our thought and imagination

[62] Dr. Hugh Ross

CHAPTER 13: Thinking outside the box

[63] Dr. Gary Zukav

[64] Gregg Braden

CHAPTER 14: Biocentrism

[65] Dr. Robert Lanza

CHAPTER 15: The "Stuff" we're made of

[66] Dr. Amit Goswami

[67] Dr. John Hagelin

[68] Dr. Phil Mason

[69] Mwanga Leonard Arapsotyo

[91]

Elizabeth Cain

[92]

Simon Yap

[93]

Matthew Robert Payne

[94]

Tylene White

[95]

Tim Heart

[96]

Jason Fugate

[97]

Lynn Hiles

[98]

Henry Harris

[99]

Bruce Harbert

[100]

Cayce Talbott

blogtalkradio

[101]

Kenneth Gaveni Shivambu

[102]

Mike Carter

[103]

Valerie Baard

[104]

Derrick Day Ministries

[105]

Jeremiah Johnson

[106]

Mark Hicks

[107]

Allen D. Gee

[108]

Enejo Adamu

[109]

Stacy Cameron

[110]

Dr. Cindye Coates

[111]

Dr. Don K. Preston

[112]

Tomsan Kattackal

[113]

Russ Lewis

[114]

Tammora Kalis

[115]

Eric Rukin

[116]

Dan Hassett

[117]

Tammy Starforth

[118]

Kagiso Mashego

[119]

Muzi Joint Heir Spirit

[120]

Bradly Taylor

[121]

Simeon Edigbe

[122]

Dr. Kay Fairchild

[123]

Steve Chukwudi Fidel

[124]

Gail Ellis

[125]

Mwanga Leonard Arapsotyo

[126]

Michael C King

[127]

Sheila Welch-Pelot

[128]

Timothy King

[129]

Francois Du Toit

[130]

David Dolejs

[131]

Angie Morales

[132]

Ernest L. Yates

[133]

Kent Lindsay

[134]

Ranjana Dickenson Sonu

[135]

Carol Anderson

[136]

Peter Wilson

[137]

Julienne Chambers

[138]

Brian Bauer

[139]

Patricia Harris

[140]

Tommy Hawk

[141]

Ted Nelson

[142]

Flora Samuel

[143]

Jean N Josh Willis

 [144]

Janet Dawson

[145]

Irene Geel

[146]

Sarah Bradt Levesque.

[147]

Kathy Hall Harris

[148]

John Senior

[149]

Christel Gast

[150]

Monty Dickerson

[151]

David Duncan

God's Covenant Journey

[152]

David Williams

[153]

Philip George

[154]

Daniel Anderson

[155]

Erna Atkins

[156]

Heather Creed

[157]

John Ogbu

[158]

Diane Maartens

[159]

Ken Etter

[160]

Sonny Hanna

[161]

Kathy Jane Nolan

[162]

David Martin Stevens

[163]

Jean-Pierre Cote

Printed in Great Britain
by Amazon